Books Kids Will Sit Still For

A Guide to Using Children's Literature for Librarians, Teachers, and Parents

By Judy Freeman

Alleyside
Press
1984

Third printing, 1984
Fourth printing, 1985
Fifth printing, 1986

Published by The Alleyside Press
Freline, Inc.
P.O. Box 889
Hagerstown, Maryland 21741

Library of Congress Cataloging in Publication Data
Freeman, Judy, 1952–
    Books kids will sit still for.
    Bibliography: p.
    Includes index.
    1. Children's literature—Bibliography. 2. Bibliography—Best books—Children's literature. 3. School libraries—Book lists. 4. School libraries—Activity programs. 5. Oral reading. I. Title.
Z1037.F847 1984 [PN1009.AI] O11'.6254 83-21414
ISBN O-913853-02-X (pbk.)

Printed in the United States of America

Quotation on page 127 from THE WAY OF THE STORYTELLER by Ruth Sawyer. Copyright 1942, 1962 by Ruth Sawyer. Copyright renewed 1970 by Ruth Sawyer. Reproduced by permission of Viking Penguin, Inc.

Dedication

To my ever-supportive husband, Izzy, for putting up with all the stories I insist on telling him, my endless rantings about children's literature, and the books and papers I've left strewn about the house. It's not easy being married to a librarian.

Table of Contents

List of Illustrations

Acknowledgments

When I began this book several years ago, my biggest hurdle was finding access to all the new books that come out like clockwork every spring and fall, for I always try to read them before buying the best ones for my library. In the past year, the following people and libraries provided invaluable assistance to me in locating and lending hundreds of titles, many of which appear on the lists within: the ever-patient and helpful Selma Rohrbacher of the New Jersey State Library, who gave me free reign in that library's outstanding resource, the Book Selection Room; Suzanne and Steve Hynes, who run the Follett Library Book Company's Valley Forge, Pa., Showroom, a literary gold mine for school librarians; and the staff of the Children's Room at the Somerset County Library in Bridgewater, N.J., for letting me have first crack at so many of their new books.

Once the book started to take shape and the mad typing began, the following kind-hearted souls unselfishly (masochistically?) offered to proofread the manuscript and make suggestions for revisions: Carol Shields, that wild Irish rose; Jane Scherer, librarian, children's book addict, and my favorite telephone companion; Lois Schochet, who took me swimming and bolstered my spirits through the beastly summer heat; and Bob and Gladys Freeman, my parents, who sustained me with scuppernong grapes and Vidalia onions during their visits.

Finally, I must acknowledge my debt to the teachers, students, and staff at Van Holten School in Bridgewater, N.J., who were my guinea pigs, helpmates, and friends. Long may they read!

Illustration by David Rose from THE TEDDY BEAR TREE by Barbara Dillon. Copyright © 1982 by Barbara Dillon. Reproduced by permission of William Morrow & Company.

Introduction
Yet Another Justification for Using Children's Literature in the Classroom

Reading aloud to a class is an enormously fulfilling undertaking for any teacher or librarian. Imagine how one of my fellow teachers felt the day she read aloud the folktale "Mr. Fox," from Minard's *Womenfolk and Fairy Tales*, and one child leapt dramatically from his seat and fervently proclaimed, "That is the best story I ever heard!"

After the same teacher entranced her students with *Mail-Order Wings* by Beatrice Gormley, she mused aloud, "Wouldn't it be fun to make your own wings?" Within a week almost every child in the class went home and constructed the most magnificent pairs of wings imaginable. The teacher took her young fledgelings on a flying jaunt around the school, and I can just bet those kids will *never* forget their experiences with that book.

Children's books, read aloud daily, profoundly affect children in ways that spelling words and phonics exercises never can. For those who claim they don't have time to read aloud, much less try any of the book-related activities that never fail to enthrall and motivate students, perhaps some priorities should be examined.

It is not enough for a librarian simply to stock books for children to read or for a teacher to teach reading with only a basal at her side. Children must be inundated with books, constantly and with a great deal of good-natured fervor, if we expect them to become more than just language decoders. Presumably, reading is far more than just a skill to be mastered with plenty of practice and a plethora of dittoes.

Reading for enjoyment is a free ticket to other cities, states, countries, or far-off worlds, and it allows us to inhabit the minds of even the most introspective characters. Just as many of us now recall rote learning of poetry with distaste and scorn, so can learning to read be unpleasant and filled with anguish for children today. We envision our students as future book consumers with discriminating tastes, aspiring to more than the latest supermarket romances; but if they read only junk as children, their adult tastes will probably be just as undemanding, if indeed they read at all. And so, we, the literary-minded teachers and librarians of the universe are in the plum position to remedy negative attitudes toward reading and to give our students the times of their lives, by immersing them in all the best children's books that our libraries and bookstores offer.

One of the easiest and most effective methods of interesting children in reading good books themselves is to read aloud to them. Children love hearing a book dramatized and brought to life while they listen. A more difficult book thus becomes accessible to everyone, not just to top readers. How do we choose these books? What do we do once we have selected them? We must cover so much material in the course of a school year. How do we justify using children's books alongside the required texts? And what educational advantages will we find?

Once you start to use children's books as a natural part of the school day, the advantages will multiply. A friend of mine, a fourth grade teacher, was indifferent to such books for years. "I'm an adult," she'd proclaim. "I don't need to read children's books. They're boring and below my literary standards." (Of course, up until that point she had never read any to test her theory.) Her classes were always fun and well-behaved in the library, but there was no spark. Finally, in desperation, I foisted upon her one book by a lunatic author, and she got hooked. Daniel Pinkwater's *Lizard Music* was the culprit, and it became the first of a series of children's books that this teacher has read with her students over the past several years. Her students were ecstatic, and a class of readers was born. The happy ending isn't over yet—each year this teacher continues to infect her students with a passion for books, using booktalks, creative dramatics, and oral reading as a daily vitamin to energize her language arts program.

This book includes a compilation of over 1,000 titles, annotated with simple plot statements and various ideas for sharing the books with children. Use it to select good books to read aloud, to build up your library collection, to recommend terrific titles for students to read on their own, and as your personal reading list to familiarize yourself with books suited for the grade levels you teach. You will also discover numerous suggestions for booktalking, storytelling, creative dramatics, using poetry, promoting writing skills, and developing comprehension and creativity, as well as ideas for using books to teach library skills, science, social studies, and language arts. Of course, reading aloud to children will create a special personal bond between you and your listeners and also give them the opportunity to appreciate varied literary styles, increase their vocabulary, develop social skills by sharing a group experience, and even nurture a sense of humor.

With over 2,000 children's books published each year, one must be extraordinarily selective when culling out the best. For each title listed, I read and rejected at least five others. I chose only those books that I have found to be winners when read aloud.

When you read a children's book, you will often find more than just a good story, although that should certainly be the most important factor in your selection. Nevertheless, each new book you read may have numerous possibilities for booktalking, storytelling, creative dramatics, writing skills, and other uses. Although the following pages detail hundreds of suggestions, you will find that once you start reading with an eye toward possible follow-up activities, you will develop a myriad of your own ideas as well that will certainly justify the presence of children's books in your daily plans.

There are children's books to appeal to every librarian, teacher, and parent, even a born cynic like my colleague. I hope that many of these titles will pique your imagination and provide you and your students with a continuing store of delight.

Illustration from HUGH PINE by Janwillem van de Wetering. Copyright © 1980 by Janwillem van de Wetering. Illustrations copyright © 1980 by Lynn Munsinger. Reproduced by permission of Houghton Mifflin Company.

Reading Aloud: Tricks of the Trade

One assumes that every librarian and teacher is an expert at reading aloud. After all, how complicated can it be? And yet, I have observed librarians reading in dull, uninterested monotones and teachers reading picture books to children who were sitting too far back to see the illustrations.

After much prodding, one reluctant teacher finally decided to read an adventure story aloud to the class. When I asked several children what they thought of the story, they said, "Oh, the book is good, but our teacher reads in *such* a boring voice!" At the same time, in a classroom across the hall, students were sliding off their chairs in anguish and pleading with the teacher to read another chapter after she calmly closed a new book at a heartstopping moment. Understandably, the second teacher's students adore being read to and are more enthusiastic and skillful readers than the students of the first teacher.

Common sense usually does the trick. Having your students sit close enough to see pictures fosters a community feeling and allows them to respond to your reading. Making frequent eye contact with your listeners as you read involves them even more, as each child will sense you are reading to him or her alone. I hold picture books up to one side, level with my shoulder, and turn my head sideways so that I can read the text while the children examine each illustration.

Your oral reading style should fit your personality. Don't feel obligated to offer a unique voice for each character or to act out each scene dramatically as you read. The words of a good read-aloud should grab your listeners even if your delivery does not equal Olivier's. When you maintain good pitch, volume, and expression as you read, your students will demonstrate their approval by their rapt attention.

One good reason for reading a new book to yourself before trying it aloud is to get a feel for the language and to hone your use of expression. If you do select a book that you have never had a chance to read before, and find yourself bored to tears as you read it to your students, don't be surprised if your listeners seem restless or uninterested. You get what you give, and to read aloud a book you dislike is pointless and unfulfilling for everyone involved.

For some books, judicious editing may help to tighten the action. If, however, you find yourself omitting long sections, paraphrasing passages, and simplifying vocabulary, perhaps your selection is just too difficult for your audience. No law says you must finish every book you start. If one title doesn't work out, there are always more to replace it.

Another editing problem may emerge when you neglect to read, or at least skim, a new book before using it with a class. In these modern times, off-color words or passages that you'd rather not read aloud will crop up at the most inopportune times. Forewarned, if you choose, you can edit these words, sentences, or even longer sections without making an issue of them, or you may choose not to select the book as a read-aloud. *How To Eat Fried Worms* by Thomas Rockwell includes the word "bastard" in the heat of an argument between two main characters. If that word bothers you, change it to "creep" or whatever you consider less offensive.

In *Buffy and Albert,* a delightful story for young children by Charlotte Pomerantz, Grandpa is annoyed with his two aging cats when one "pees" on the floor. Anyone with a dog or cat knows what that's like, and children accept it without question (though often with original descriptions of their own pets' bathroom habits). If you consider the language to be inappropriate, alter it. After all you have the final say over what you read aloud.

On a grander scale, in an uproarious chapter in Roald Dahl's *The BFG,* the Big Friendly Giant explains to Sophie, the little orphan girl he has kidnapped, about whizzpoppers, or what happens to him after he drinks the downwardly fizzing drink, frobscottle. If you are not prepared for the inevitable flatulence jokes from your third or fourth graders, perhaps you will want to avoid this book, although you will be missing a story filled with the most hilariously convoluted language since Casey Stengel.

After you finish a new book, make it available to your children to read on their own. A quick test of memory is an enjoyable way to decide who gets to borrow it first. Just say, "I'm thinking of a character (or place, or event, or word) from the story. Guess it and the book is yours." Make your choice difficult enough that eager contenders will mentally review the story, and you can measure by their answers just how much they recall.

A Chapter or Two May Suffice

For upper grade children there is a middle ground between booktalking and reading the whole book aloud—reading just the first chapter of a book they won't be able to resist. Often in the library, I'll settle in with, say, a fifth grade class, and I'll read through the beginning of a captivating story like Lynne Reid Banks's *The Indian in the Cupboard*, in which a tiny plastic toy Indian is inadvertently brought to life by Omri, a nine–year–old English boy. Or, as Thanksgiving creeps up in mid-November, I'll try *The Hoboken Chicken Emergency* by Daniel Pinkwater, and listen to the students cluck in amusement as they meet Henrietta, the two–hundred–and–sixty–six pound live superchicken that Arthur brings home for the big meal.

The first chapter is often enough to get students hooked. As long as you can leave them hanging in suspense, they'll demand to know what comes next. It's cruel, I realize, but it's for their own good. The next thing you know, the little scamps will be sneaking a read during math, and you'll actually need to scold them for inappropriate bookishness.

Not just any first chapter will do. Be selective when searching for the perfect grabber—a book full of action and the unusual twist. Since not all first chapters are consummate specimens of their genres, keep a sharp lookout for the self-sufficient chapter that is complete, in addition to the one that keeps you contemplating the ultimate outcome. For example, *Into the Painted Bear Lair* by Pamela Stearns is perfect for grades three to five. It concerns Gregory, a boy who ignores a "Keep Out" sign in the toy store only to end up in the living room of a live, full-sized, intelligent, boy-hungry bear. Luckily, Sir Rosemary comes to the rescue in full armour, as your children beseech you for more. That's when you raffle off the book, or, if you are a soft touch, you keep reading.

To get you started, here is a hodgepodge of books that start out wonderfully and get even better. Dip into a chapter or two with your young charges.

First-Chapter-or-Two Read-Alouds for Grades 2—4

Try the first two or three short chapters of Catherine Storr's *Clever Polly and the Stupid Wolf,* in which a nitwit of a wolf tries every fairy tale-related trick that he knows to gobble up his succulent young target. Speaking of eating, *How To Eat Fried Worms* by Thomas Rockwell is enough to put even the hardiest gourmet off her feed for a while, as Billy accepts a fifty–dollar bet to eat one worm a day—a night-crawler, no less—for fifteen days. Your students won't even flinch, but if you start feeling queasy, stop reading after the first worm. (CAUTION—DO NOT READ BEFORE LUNCH!)

The first two chapters in Ann Cameron's *The Stories Julian Tells* are delightful. In the first, Julian and his little brother Huey accidentally eat the lemon pudding that their father has concocted, and they must face much whipping and beating as their punishment. No, this book does not advocate child abuse; the wily father instructs his apprehensive sons to whip the egg whites and beat the other ingredients together to replace the missing pudding! In chapter two, Julian tells his gullible little brother that a catalog is a book filled with cats that will leap out and plant his garden for him. I keep a Burpee catalog in school to show what a real seed catalog looks like. (What, no Burpee catalog? Write to W. Atlee Burpee Co., Warminster, PA 18974, and they'll send you one free.)

Sideways Stories from Wayside School by Louis Sachar is a bizarre tale of the top–floor class in a school that was inadvertently built thirty stories high. In the first chapter, the mean teacher turns most of her students into apples, only to find herself transformed as well.

Although the entire book is riotously funny, the April Fools' Day chapter in *Peter Potts* by Clifford Hicks makes a perfect climax to the usual April 1 antics that your students are sure to pull. Don't read it until the first week in April, or you will find yourself fielding one practical joke after another from your overzealous pranksters.

The gentle humor and matter-of-fact charm of Janwillem Van de Wetering's *Hugh Pine* will make you want to drive straight to the Maine woods. Hugh Pine, one intelligent hat-and-coat-clad porcupine among his lesser-brained associates, must find a way to reduce traffic fatalities among his slow-moving relatives.

Chapters from Sobol's "Encyclopedia Brown" mystery series are good training for future Holmesian sleuths because listeners must use logic and deductive reasoning to crack each of the ten cases per book. Detailed solutions are appended for those of us who are not as swift as the clever young son of Idaville's police chief. In the same vein, try the "Einstein Anderson" science sleuth series by Seymour Simon.

For good Halloween fare, start *What's Happened to Harry* by Barbara Dillon and see if you will be permitted to stop once young Harry has been turned into a poodle by the malevolent witch who takes over his body.

First-Chapter-or-Two Read-Alouds for Grades 4—6

From four books of short stories, I've culled four favorites. The title story in Ruth Ainsworth's collection *The Phantom Carousel*, about a boy and the special wooden horse he rides at a local fair, is haunting, with a suitably mystical and touching ending. Alfred Slote's title story in *The Devil Rides with Me* is about an earnest young skier who makes an inadvertent bargain with Satan himself. One might need to watch *Masterpiece Theater* to perfect the Cockney accent of Michael Fish, the professional fingersmith in Roald Dahl's story "The Hitchhiker," from the collection *The Wonderful Story of Henry Sugar*. Even without the accent, your students will give diligent attention to this tale of two men who run afoul of the law. And finally, in Lloyd Alexander's book, *The Town Cats and Other Tales*, you will have a dramatic field day imitating the clucking, tight-fisted shopkeeper outwitted by a cunning feline in "The Cat and the Golden Egg."

Lloyd Alexander's books plead to be read aloud, as anyone who has read *The First Two Lives of Lukas-Kasha* can attest. After that lazy bounder Lukas pays his penny to a marketplace conjurer and is dunked in a pail of water, he finds himself inexplicably drowning in a real ocean by an unfamiliar shore.

Rufus finds his family's farm veritably drowning in cash after a leprechaun grants his wish for *All the Money in the World*, a clever yarn of greed and trickery by Bill Brittain. This talented author evokes the fairy tale aura of misty New England in *Devil's Donkey*, about the calamitous consequences a young unbeliever faces when he cuts a branch off the forbidden witches' tree.

On the lighter side, meet *Veronica Ganz*, a girl with a mission. As the self-proclaimed class bully, she feels obligated to pound the tar out of every newcomer, including that sassy little shrimp, Peter Wedermeyer. The problem, as author Marilyn Sachs so masterfully tells us, is that Peter is not one bit overawed by Veronica's brawn. "Veronica Ganz doesn't wear pants," he taunts her, and she swears vengeance.

Most people think the story of the Pied Piper is only a fairy tale, but author Gloria Skurzynski travelled all the way to Hamelin, Germany, to research her riveting fiction version of *What Happened in Hamelin*. Based on the actual events of 1284 when all the children from the rat-infested town were led away, the book is narrated by Geist, the orphaned baker's apprentice, who is befriended by the piper and is ultimately left behind.

Let the above titles start you on a reading binge, but be sure to diversify your literary agenda. If you persist in always reading only the first chapter, you will be depriving your children of completing the grand tour, like eating whipped cream all the time without ever tasting the hot fudge and the mocha chip ice cream underneath. Vary the fare, alternating from booktalking to reading single chapters and entire books of all genres. Even the best books get monotonous if you stick to just one type. Try some historical, some hysterical, a pinch of sci-fi, a sip of fantasy, a few stray animal tales, a couple contemporary, a soupçon of mystery, and an adventure or two. Stretch your students and yourself as well.

Illustration from the jacket cover by Lawrence Di Fiori of A TOAD FOR TUESDAY by Russell E. Erickson. Illustration copyright © 1974 by Lawrence Di Fiori. Reproduced by permission of Lothrop, Lee & Shepard Books (A Division of William Morrow & Company).

Booktalking

Obviously, no teacher or librarian could read aloud all the books on any one grade level. (The texts for kindergarten through second grade, however, are brief enough to facilitate the completion of dozens in the course of a year.) If you would like to familiarize your students with great numbers of books, and stir up unquenchable interest at the same time, start booktalking.

When I go to the movies, I love to watch the coming attractions. In a very few minutes I can discover what the next new movies can offer and decide if they are worth a return visit to the theater. Booktalks are the educator's equivalent of coming attractions. After just one minute of plugging, you will have 15 eager children pleading with you to let them read the book you just described. It takes very little time to prepare and deliver several one-minute booktalks, and your students will be passing the books around to one another for weeks.

Anybody can booktalk. You do it every time you recommend a book to someone, and certainly there is no trick to that. Yet, when I've conducted booktalking workshops or courses for teachers or librarians, some people always say, "Well, sure, *you* can do booktalks. But I don't have the (select one): time...patience...talent...guts...skill...knowledge...need...student interest...to do it myself." Horsefeathers! Booktalking is a cinch, so long as you don't allow yourself to become overawed by it.

Here are ten easy and painless steps for prospective booktalkers to follow.
1. Select some hilarious, exciting, terrific, terrifying, mystifying, thrilling, heartrending quality titles (including non-fiction and poetry as well as fiction), that you have read and that are on your students' various and varied interest and reading levels.
2. Skim through the first third of each book to re-familiarize yourself with plot, characters, and setting, all the while looking for short action-packed scenes to entice your students.
3. Keeping your own personal platitudes to a minimum ("You'll just *love* this book..." is unnecessary, because if you didn't think they'd love it, you wouldn't take the time to talk about it), compose a short—30–second to

ten–minute—description of a dramatic incident, a plot overview, or a character study that will involve your listeners and make them eager to know more.

4. The longer your booktalk is, the more detailed it will be. I like to look for a complete episode that I can tell as a story, although a short description fits the bill perfectly for some books. A long booktalk does not tell too much. If you find yourself explaining what happened to every character and revealing the second half of the book, give yourself a good kick and cut it short. After all, why should anyone read the book if you've already told everything that happens?

5. Try to duplicate the flavor of the original prose in your retelling. If you are describing a particularly funny, riveting, terrifying, or poignant moment, the audience will want to experience each emotion. Be dramatic when the scene calls for it, but don't overdo it. The students will want to focus on the story, not your histrionics. If it fits, you can include a key passage to read aloud. Mark it with a paperclip on the side so that you won't have to fumble for the right page.

6. Learn the names of your characters. If you get stuck, as we all do now and again, casually open to the flap of the book where, if you are lucky, such vital statistics will reside. If not, idly leaf through a few pages until you find what you need. The children won't know it's not part of your planned speech unless you tell them, so don't tell them. They don't need to know all your tricks.

7. Practice your booktalk. (I sometimes rehearse new talks while standing before the large round mirror that hangs over my bathroom sink. Woe be to the unfortunate person who needs to use the facilities when I'm working!) While practicing, be on the lookout to correct any rocking or swaying, nervous and unnecessary hand movements, mumbling, lack of eye contact, and inappropriate nail biting. If you are unsure or jittery, don't advertise it—overcome it. You teach because you like to perform in front of children; take advantage of the natural reverence in which children hold you, and don't be afraid of making a donkey's hindquarters of yourself.

8. When you give your booktalk to your students, make sure that you clearly state the title and author of each

book and show the cover at some point during your discourse. Distribute the books, after you finish, to the children who want them. Try raffling the books for a change, by picking a number, letter, month, state, river, or color for the children to guess. The winners will be as pleased as if they had won the million–dollar lottery.

9. Keep a record of the talks you give so that you don't forget and try to sell the same book twice. It's a good idea to record the reading and interest levels and the types of books you use so that you can keep your selection varied. Don't worry—the more you booktalk, the easier it gets.

10. Teach your students to booktalk. They love to do it, and it spreads the literary wealth so much farther. Second graders are not too young; even kindergartners and first graders can tell about what they have read without revealing the endings. Have your students share their booktalks with other classes. You just might spark a reading revolution in your school.

Types of Booktalks

Short Talks

You can tackle several types of booktalks. The fastest and the easiest is the short one to two minute talk. If you do three or four at a time, you'll have spent very little time introducing more books than you would use in several months. Following are two examples of short talks you might give to fourth, fifth, or sixth graders:

Timothy Carpenter was only eleven when Great Aunt Emma came to visit his family. On January 14, the doorbell rang, and there she was—all 5′1″ of her. Not only had Tim never met her, he never even knew he *had* a great aunt. Neither did his mother, apparently, until Great Aunt Emma went up to her, stared intently into her eyes, and said, "You remember me, Millie!" *Grinny* by Nicholas Fisk, is Tim's diary of the three months Great Aunt Emma spent with the Carpenter family, detailing his younger sister Beth's increasing suspicion and dread that Great Aunt Emma was not who she seemed—that perhaps she was not even human.

During the school year, her name is Betsy Kendell, but *In Summertime It's Tuffy*. She's been to three summer camps in three years, and this summer she's at Camp Ma-Sha-Na, in a bunk with a counselor and five other girls, getting in trouble on the very first day. Tuffy and her bunkmates are typical campers: there's Natalie who's boy crazy, Adele who's allergic to everything, Iris who plays guitar and reads up on black magic, Debbie the food freak, and Verna the cleaning nut. If you've ever been to summer camp, or if you'd like to see just what you've been missing, *In Summertime It's Tuffy* by Judie Angell will tell you all you need to know.

Illustration from THE PHANTOM TOLLBOOTH by Norton Juster. Text copyright © 1961 by Norton Juster. Illustrations copyright © 1961 by Jules Feiffer. Published by Random House Young Books, Inc.

Theme Booktalks

Next, try a theme booktalk. By selecting books with a common thread (loneliness, food, pets, jealousy, fear, new neighbors), you can link them together in your presentation, almost like telling a long segmented story, with an introduction and a wind-up ending. In the following booktalk designed for fourth graders, the reading levels range from third through fifth grades, with genres including humor, adventure, and mystery. The theme loosely connecting all four books, which otherwise have very little in common, is "Trees."

Trees Booktalk

(Introduction)

Now that spring is here, I find myself waiting for the trees outside the library to bloom. That's how I know summer is really on its way.

(Ease into Book 1)

Imagine what it would be like if all the trees near your house stayed green and leafy, even through the snows of January. When the Finch family moved into their new house, that's just what they found. Even on the coldest days of the year, flowers bloomed outside their house and snow melted immediately. You see, the Finches had a volcano steaming in their basement. They never needed to worry about heating bills because the temperature in the house always hovered around 80°. For a while, the volcano seemed harmless enough. Read Roger Drury's book *The Finches' Fabulous Furnace* to discover what happened during that fateful year when the volcano started to grow.

(Book 2)

Actually, it was one snow-covered winter tree that almost cost Warton his life in the book *A Toad for Tuesday* by Russell E. Erickson. Warton lived in a snug house underground with his brother Morton. The two toads spent a cozy winter feasting on Morton's baked goodies until Warton took it into his head to venture out in the cold and snow with a basket of beetle brittle for their Aunt Toolia. Nothng Morton could say would discourage this foolhardy notion, even though toads never go outside in freezing weather. Warton was so determined, he made himself a pair of skis from oak tree roots and ski poles from porcupine quills, and then he set out on his journey. He was not even halfway when disaster struck. A hungry owl spied Warton whizzing by, snatched him away, and deposited him in a filthy hideaway at the top of a tall oak tree. Warton was a prisoner—until Tuesday, that is—for Tuesday was the nasty owl's birthday, and that owl planned to eat one nice, juicy toad on that day to celebrate!

(Book 3)

Warton the toad wanted only to escape from that tree. But Rob, in the book *The View from the Cherry Tree* by Willo Davis Roberts, used the cherry tree as his escape from everyone else around him. You see, Rob's sister, Darcy, was getting married, and the whole household was in an uproar, getting ready for the big day. It seemed that no matter what Rob did, he was in the way. The cherry tree was one place he could hide, alone, without anyone nagging or pestering him. Up in the tree, he also had a perfect opportunity to spy, unseen, on everyone below: on his father and uncle arguing, on his sister and her fiance, and even on old lady Calloway, the nasty next door neighbor who made his life miserable with her scolding and surly threats. It was in the cherry tree that Rob happened to witness the sight of an unidentified pair of man's hands that pushed the old woman out her first-floor window. Rob watched in horror as the cord of the old woman's ever-present binoculars caught on a tree branch, causing her to strangle to death. An accident, everyone said. Only Rob knew the truth—that old lady Calloway had been murdered—and no one seemed to believe his story . . . except for the anonymous killer.

(Conclusion)

As you can see from these books, trees can be places of danger, as well as shelter, and shade. So why don't you borrow one of these copies, settle into a nice, cozy spot under an oak, or even a cherry tree, and have a good read?

Naturally, many other books would tie into a "Trees" theme booktalk just as well. For grades two to four, possibilities include Barbara Dillon's *The Teddy Bear Tree*, Clyde Robert Bulla's King Arthur story, *The Sword in the Tree*, and James Flora's tale of a vine run amok, *The Great Green Turkey Creek Monster*. For grades three to six, the following books would also work nicely: Philippa Pearce's fantasy *Tom's Midnight Garden;* Lloyd Alexander's *The Wizard in the Tree;* Sonia Levitin's *Jason and the Money Tree,* about a boy who plants a ten–dollar bill; *The Magic Orange Tree,* a collection of Haitian folktales by Diane Wolkstein; and Jean George's *My Side of the Mountain,* a back-to-the-wilderness survival tale.

Many books you select have a multitude of theme tie-ins. For instance, *The Finches' Fabulous Furnace* also deals with explosions, moving, seasons, and the Fourth of July; *A Toad for Tuesday* touches on sports, flying, reptiles and amphibians, and making friends; *The View from the Cherry Tree* covers sibling relationships, murder, mystery, cats or pets, spying, and weddings or family get-togethers. Your chosen themes can be as broad or as limited as you like.

Longer Booktalks

Long talks are often based on just one or two books, described in more detail than in short talks. Lasting from three to ten minutes, long talks examine an entire episode or series of scenes in a book, resulting in greater emotional involvement on the parts of both teller and listener.

Bunnicula by James and Deborah Howe makes a delightful longer talk, as you describe the circumstances under which the Monroe family found that little bunny (on a seat at a Dracula movie) and took it home to Chester the cat and Harold the dog (the narrator of the tale), who discovered that the rabbit was, in fact, a vegetarian vampire.

Or try Barbara Brooks Wallace's gothic mystery thriller, *Peppermints in the Parlor,* about an orphaned poor-little-rich girl who is forced to work as a servant upon arrival at her beloved aunt's mansion in turn-of-the-century San Francisco.

Author Booktalks

One more type of booktalk is the author talk, in which you use more than one title by a single author. Often you can booktalk a series, like Lloyd Alexander's Prydain Chronicles (*The Book of Three, The Black Cauldron, The Castle of Lyr, Taran Wanderer,* and *The High King*), C.S. Lewis's Narnia books (*The Lion, the Witch and the Wardrobe, The Magician's Nephew,* etc.), or "The Great Brain" books by John D. Fitzgerald.

Beverly Cleary's "Ramona" books are still the greatest, and the egg-cracking scene in *Ramona Quimby, Age 8* is one of the best examples of booktalking nirvana that I know. Jean Van Leeuwen's mouse trilogy consisting of *The Great Cheese Conspiracy, The Great Christmas Kidnapping Caper,* and *The Great Rescue Operation* ties with Cleary's "Ralph" books (*The Mouse and the Motorcycle, Runaway Ralph,* and *Ralph S. Mouse*) for children's devotion and affection.

Then there is Robert Newton Peck's "Soup" series, with so many funny describable incidents, it's almost impossible to choose just a few. The books of several other authors make magnificent topics for author booktalks; Scott Corbett, Sid Fleischman, Betsy Byars, Daniel Pinkwater, Ellen Conford, Roald Dahl, Alfred Slote, Patricia Beatty, E.B. White, and John Bellairs are some of my personal favorites.

Booktalk Record-Keeping

If you are the type of person who keeps good records of what you do, then begin a file of booktalk cards so that you will not have to start from scratch each year. *Witch's Sister* by Phyllis Reynolds Naylor makes a marvelously terrifying long talk, and once you record it, you can easily remember the entire talk a year later by just referring to your file card.

Sample Booktalk File Card

Themes: Witchcraft, Siblings, Suspense
Grade Level: 4–6
Title: *Witch's Sister* by Phyllis Reynolds Naylor
     Atheneum, 1979.
Blurb: After Lynn and her best friend Mouse investigate, they become convinced that Lynn's 14–year–old sister is learning witchcraft from Mrs. Tuggle, a deceptively sweet old lady who lives up the hill.
Characters: Lynn Morley (12 years old, precise, imaginative)
    Mouse Beasley (Lynn's best friend, timid, sloppy dresser)
    Judith Morley (Lynn's older sister, suspected of witchcraft)
    Mrs. Tuggle (English, older, sinister, a witch)
    Mrs. Morley (Lynn's mother, children's book author)
    Stevie Morley (Lynn's 6–year–old brother)
Booktalk: 1. Lynn suspects her sister, Judith, of learning witchcraft from Mrs. Tuggle. List reasons Lynn gives: pp. 3, 5, 15.

2. Lynn and Mouse spy on Judith and Mrs. Tuggle, only to see them sticking pins in a doll: pp. 35–38.
3. Include mention of two other titles in trilogy: *Witch Water* and *The Witch Herself.*

Most of the books on the read-aloud lists for grades two through six make wonderful booktalks with a bit of planning and a touch of the old soft-shoe. Your students will let you know by their reading how much they appreciate your efforts.

Illustration from LAZY TOMMY PUMPKINHEAD. Story and pictures by William Pène du Bois. Copyright © 1966 by William Pène du Bois. Reproduced by permission of Harper & Row, Publishers, Inc.

Creative Dramatics and Children's Literature

In the annotations of the read-aloud lists, I have purposely included brief suggestions when titles lend themselves to follow-up activities. Many of the books are perfect to use for creative drama, from narrative pantomime to improvised dialogue, and I can think of no better way to make a story leap to life for children. You know the usual scene: You finish reading a story aloud and ask a few innocent interpretive questions. Two or three students come up with enthusiastic insights, while the rest fidget. Finally, one outspoken tyke looks you dead in the pupils and says, "Can we get our library books now?" Aargh!

Now zoom in for this bit of reversal: You've just finished Brinton Turkle's *Do Not Open,* a startling story of a woman who calmly outwits the terrifying creature she has released from a bottle. Instead of asking, "How and why does the voice of the creature change from bottle to freedom?" or "Was Miss Moody scared of the monster?" have the class break into pairs—Miss Moody versus the still-bottled creature. Allow them several minutes of debating time for each "monster" to convince each doubting but curious Miss Moody to release it from the bottle. Then have them switch characters and have each Miss Moody trick each creature into becoming a mouse. While the pairs are arguing, look around, but don't impose yourself on any discussions. You will be able to tell which pairs are involved easily enough. Afterward, get back together as a group, and ask the children how it went. *Now* you will hear them answer questions eagerly and talk non-stop about how each character responded to the situation.

Using creative drama to extend a story allows children to develop new criteria for interpreting characters and understanding their actions. As a group activity, creative drama provides children with the freedom to try new ideas without fear of ridicule. All the comprehension skills booklets in the world won't help students to fathom cause and effect the way acting out a story will.

Narrative Pantomime

While you may feel self-conscious and unsure the first time you lead your crew in a narrative pantomime, those feelings will soon flee when you note the actors' ecstatic faces and hear them exclaim, "Let's do it again!" After reading a story aloud, you can usually complete a narrative pantomime tour de force in less than ten minutes. More complex productions take longer, but if you start out simply, you will find the activities easy to complete successfully.

Narrative pantomime—narrating the events from a story, either word-for-word or self-edited to fit the situation—is the easiest technique to direct and perform. Look for a story or episode with scads of action, a simple plot, and little or no dialogue. Set up guidelines for your students; when you clap your hands, say, "Freeze," or bang a drum, all children are to stop immediately and listen. Practice that with them so that they know what to expect. Any child who cannot follow along without "cutting up" should sit out until he or she is ready to participate. Children will want to be part of all the action, and they will simmer down fast after you calmly sit them down to watch for a spell. To prevent problems, have the children space themselves so that they are not within touching distance of anyone else.

In a narrative pantomime, the leader narrates the story while the participants act out the words. Editing is essential in many cases to speed up the action so that children are not standing around, pondering their next moves. You will find, however, that most children will be quite un-self-conscious once they get involved and realize that no one is watching them for mistakes or to criticize. Each person becomes too wrapped up in the story to take notice of anyone else. When editing, omit the talky sections, condense the time span if necessary, and cut or add additional description to make the action flow more logically and sequentially.

During the month of April, any class would enjoy hearing David Cleveland's *The April Rabbits*. As the month progresses, Robert keeps seeing more and more bunnies doing the strangest things, such as tap dancing, flying, playing basketball, and singing on the garage roof. Once you've shared this giddy little romp with your young whippersnappers, reread it aloud while they act the parts of the rabbits in unison. The only additions you might need to make are in places where the action is shown in the illustration rather than in the text. "Eight rabbits left their bikes in the driveway on the eighth" might profit from the addition, ". . . and then they hid in a tree."

After you've acted out a story, if the children are enthusiastic, run through it again. It's a good idea to offer them suggestions for improvement—no personal comments, just some new ideas on which to focus. For example, "This time, let's try to make our rabbits seem even sneakier. When you play basketball, paddle canoes, or ride bikes, make each action seem *real*."

Usually no character development occurs in simple narrative pantomime; it's but a literal interpretation of a story. Yet after you finish, you will find that your students have a sharper sense of setting and sequence. Sit them down and ask what parts they liked doing most and why. Give each child a chance to respond.

Acting out picture books is enjoyed by all ages. When I was introducing the parts of a catalog card to my third graders, I first read aloud the picture book *Humphrey the Dancing Pig* by Arthur Getz, about a pig who decides to dance until he is as thin as the cat. He tries the hula, rock and roll, gymnastics, ballet and other dances, until he is so lithe, the farmer puts him to work catching vermin. After discussing the parts of the book including author, illustrator, publisher, copyright date, and call number, we constructed a large oaktag author card based on the title page. Then, to unwind from our labors, we acted out the story; children all played the part of Humphrey, while I was the farmer/narrator. From the text, I condensed a week's worth of dancing into the time frame of one day and ended the play with Humphrey asleep in his corn crib, fat and contented once again. When possible, end an active production like this with the characters sitting or sleeping, to give everyone a chance to settle down.

Other picture books adaptable to narrative pantomime can be found lurking in the lists ahead. Here are just a few worth trying. *Talking Without Words* by Marie Hall Ets is about non-verbal communication. Younger students can act out each situation with the appropriate motions. One typical page reads, "'Come here!' I say to my dog. But I don't say it with words. I just click my tongue and pat my knee and he comes."

While doing an author talk on the delicious books of Arnold Lobel, I showed my second graders *Mouse Tales*, explaining how Papa Mouse told his boys seven bedtime stories, one for each mouse. The fifth story, "The Journey," is about a mouse who drives, roller skates, tramps, runs, and walks all the way to his mother's house, and we acted it out, giggling all the way home. We made the trip twice in five minutes—nothing fancy, just fun.

Catastrophe Cat by Dennis Panek has very few words, so to act it out, you must supply a running narration. Young children love all the havoc he wreaks, and you'll appreciate the calm ending, with the cat back home at last, snoozing away.

How I Hunted the Little Fellows, an autobiographical story by Russian author Boris Zhitkov, makes a fascinating drama for grades three to five, with some careful editing. Boria convinces himself that little men live inside the model ship that his grandmother has forbidden him to touch. After reading the story aloud, ask your listeners why Boria thought there were little fellows in the ship, and what they—your students—would have done in his place. Then, ask them to imagine that Boria's fantasy was true and to become the little fellows hiding in the steamer, dramatizing the action as you read it aloud. Before starting, you will need to mark the pertinent passages, starting with:

> "I was sure that the cabin door could open and that the little fellows were living inside. . . . I waited to see if one looked out the window. Surely they would look out from time to time. When nobody was home, they probably went out on deck and climbed up the rope ladders to the masts. But if they heard the slightest noise, then— whisk—quick as mice, they would duck back into the cabin, crouch down, and keep quiet."

Then read the description of the little fellows chopping the candy and the one that details their sitting all day on benches, shoulder to shoulder, until they sneak on deck and leave their footprints on the ink-soaked mat. Next comes some real action as Boria shakes the steamer upside down while the little fellows hold on tight.

For an understanding of the destruction that he causes, have the students now become Boria as you read aloud the passage of his dismantling the boat, up to his despairing realization that the little fellows do not, in fact, exist. Afterward, sit back down and discuss why he reacted the way he did. Finally, students can write or tell about the worst things *they* ever did.

Illustration (and text quoted on page 23) from HOW I HUNTED THE LITTLE FELLOWS by Boris Zhitkov, translated by Djemma Bider, illustrated by Paul O. Zelinsky. Translation copyright © 1979 by Djemma Bider. Illustrations copyright © 1979 by Paul O. Zelinsky. Reproduced by permission of Dodd, Mead & Company, Inc.

If you've ever read the humorous 1889 English novel *Three Men in a Boat,* written by Jerome K. Jerome, and even if you haven't, don't miss Wallace Tripp's riotous rabbity excerpt entitled *My Uncle Podger.* Since the humor is filled with typically British understatement, I often wonder if the narration, concerning inept Uncle Podger's all-day attempt to hang a picture, is over the children's heads. A narrative pantomime, in which everybody re-enacts the gentleman rabbit's struggles, clarifies the funny parts, rendering them even more tickling. You will need to perform some judicious editing so that Uncle P. will remain the center of the action. Most of us are acquainted with at least one similar pompous buffoon, and the acting can lead into an entertaining character analysis.

For grades four to six, give Paddington his time in the tub. *A Bear Called Paddington* by Michael Bond contains a marvelous scene in which that bumbling bear takes his very first tub bath (pp. 29–32). Students will love bailing out of the flood with their imaginary floppy hats.

When you are in the middle of a booktalk, acting out a segment is a novel twist that involves everyone. As you relate the bizarre experiences of Andrea in Beatrice Gormley's *Mail-Order Wings,* your students, grades four to six, can pantomime applying the wings to their shoulders, not being able to remove them, and practicing flying with them.

All ages delight in adventure-prone Grandpa from James Stevenson's *Could Be Worse* and *We Can't Sleep.* Who wouldn't like riding on a shark's fin, weight-lifting a walrus, or riding a paper airplane home to bed? Try it and see.

Don't neglect poetry as another splendid source. "True Story" from Shel Silverstein's *Where the Sidewalk Ends* allows students to enact a cowboy's perilous adventures, and even to die at the end. With young children, try ordinary nursery rhymes such as "Jack Be Nimble," "Little Miss Muffet," and "Humpty Dumpty." For "Little Miss Muffet," divide the class into pairs: Miss Muffet versus the spider. "Humpty Dumpty" can be done as a group, with half comprising the giant egg and the other half, soldiers.

Using Pantomime in Pairs and as a Group

Narrative pantomime need not always be a solo venture, with all children playing the same part. Children can work in pairs or as a group, depending on the story to be performed. Children often find pairs pantomime satisfying because they can switch roles midway and experience two characters for the price of one.

Pairs Pantomime

In James Daugherty's *Andy and the Lion,* the updated confrontation between Andy and the thorny-pawed lion provides a perfect theatrical interlude. Before acting out the scene, students need to be prepped to avoid the pitfalls of acting out of character. They will need to discuss how the boy can be startled by the hidden lion's tail, how boy and lion can chase each other around an imaginary rock without being caught, how Andy can carefully de-thorn the lion's paw, and how the lion can pretend to lick Andy's face. Miraculous solutions to these problems will be suggested. It's a good idea to have a pair demonstrate feasible possibilities. One child may show how the lion could crouch, with one hand or foot extended to suggest the tail; when the lion moves this "tail," the other child will jump back in alarm. (If there are an odd number, don't hesitate to designate a threesome with two lions or two Andys. One child may even want to play the dog.)

When my second graders acted out the chapter, I allowed no chairs or tables to be used as props, yet the children were genuinely startled by how believable the scene was to them. One boy exclaimed, "I was really scared when that lion twitched his tail!" After the first time, I made a few suggestions for improvement—"This time, get a better grip on the thorn before you pull so that both of you really feel it when it finally comes out."—had them switch parts, and we went through it again. The text needs no editing; it has action and just the right amount of dramatic tension. Afterward, when we discussed their favorite moments, they were at no loss for words.

For pairs pantomime, look for stories with dynamic duos; James Marshall's "George and Martha" or Arnold Lobel's "Frog and Toad" tales are fine examples. Mirra Ginsburg's *The Chick and the Duckling* fits the bill for the younger set, as does any complete version of "Old Mother Hubbard and Her Dog."

For longer fiction, again you must keep one eye trained for pertinent passages. One good choice is Christine Nostlinger's *Konrad,* about Mrs. Bartolotti, an eccentric weaver who unexpectedly finds herself the parent of a factory-canned seven-year-old son. After the mailman delivers a large parcel, she removes the wrappings and extricates a huge gleaming can with a ring-pull. Opening the can, she is shocked by the contents: a crumpled dwarf-like creature who, after Mrs. B. douses him with the enclosed nutrient solution, is transformed into a perfectly normal child. In performing the pairs pantomime of Konrad and Mrs. Bartolotti, the child who plays Konrad really has two parts: first as the can and then as the contents of that can. Caution your students to perform without hamming it up, as Mrs. B. must show an emotional reaction of surprise and shock whereas Konrad must remain stoic as the container.

Most children love to try mirror exercises. Use them with *Winnie-the-Pooh* as he does his daily stretching exercises before the mirror, or with John Himmelman's *Talester the Lizard,* in which Talester's best friend is his own reflection. You have probably seen the Marx Brothers or the "I Love Lucy" episodes in which Groucho and Harpo or Lucy and Harpo meet while costumed identically and mirror each other's actions. With your class, have the pairs face each other; as one child begins to move, the partner must attempt to mirror faithfully every action. Start out slowly, then have everyone speed up a bit. Try it yourself—it's trickier than it looks!

Group Pantomime

Now that you've tried solo and pairs pantomime, group pantomime is the next logical step. With Alexei Tolstoi's *The Great Big Enormous Turnip,* ask for volunteers to play the turnips, the old man and woman, the granddaughter, the dog, the cat, and the mouse. Cast more than one child for each role as needed so that everyone can take part. Warm up by having all children become turnips, sown from seeds, leaves peeking above the earth, and growing toward the sun. Pretend to pull their leaves so that they lean precariously, but stay in the soil. Then narrate the whole story as the group acts it out. This is the simplest sort of group story to act out because children have no real need of dialogue and the story is linear, with each new character simply following the others.

The group can also work together to form a unit, as in *Lazy Tommy Pumpkinhead* by William Pene du Bois, in which a lazy boy depends on machines to wake, wash, dress, and feed him. Have students become those machines with each child or small group performing the functions of their choice. With you in charge of the "controls," have your "machines" speed up or slow down and request accompanying sound effects for each function. The robot factory in Alfred Slote's *My Robot Buddy* can be created similarly, as students band together to manufacture the various parts of the robots. Assembly line pantomimes are always interesting because each child's actions must be interdependent of those of the other children.

Using Sound

Narrative pantomime is usually silent because children must listen carefully for various cues. In many stories, children need to use their voices as well, to mimic the sounds that enrich the tellings. A whimsical story like *Peace at Last* by Jill Murphy would fall flat if the listeners didn't join in on all the snoring, ticking, dripping, and tweeting noises that keep Mr. Bear from getting his forty winks.

After I read *Peace at Last* to a first grade, we recorded a cassette tape of the sound effects in sequence. We all love/hate to hear ourselves on tape because we always sound different somehow. Children are fascinated with identifying their own recorded voices, and the first graders listened very carefully to directions so that their output would be a success. First we discussed the order of the noises and practiced how a dripping faucet or ticking clock might sound. I purposely did not offer my own interpretations so that the children would be free to devise their own sounds and decide who would do each one. After a short rehearsal, we taped in sequence, turing off the tape recorder after each noise. Everyone joined in on the cat and bird choruses; otherwise, from one to three vocalists composed each sound. When we finished the tape, we then acted out the complete story in pantomime, with each child playing the part of Mr. Bear while I narrated. As each noise came up in the story, I would switch on our recorded tape, after which the multitude of "bears" would exclaim, "Oh, NO! I can't stand THIS."

Certain stories lend themselves to sound effects. Rolf Myller's *A Very Noisy Day* was written for that purpose, encompassing all the noises a dog might encounter in a day. George Shannon's story *Lizard's Song*, about a bear who can't remember the words, has an oft-repeated chorus that *must* be sung for the best effect. When reading aloud Judith

Viorst's book *My Mama Says There Aren't Any Zombies, Ghosts, Vampires, Creatures, Demons, Fiends, Goblins, or Things* (a cataloguer's nightmare if ever there was one), it's ever so much scarier if your listeners make all the accompanying creepy noises described so graphically in the text. Speaking of chills, *King of the Cats* by Paul Galdone, a folktale about a gravedigger who witnesses a cat funeral procession, is interspersed with harrowing miaows that should be cried in unison.

Sometimes just a segment of a story or novel is appropriate for a sound-effects interlude. Younger students will want to "ba-loop" through the clam concert in *Clams Can't Sing* by James Stevenson. One second grade teacher and class were so enamored with their cacophany, they made a twenty-minute "Morning Sounds at the Beach" tape which they sent to the author, who wrote back agreeing that clams really *can* sing.

No, you don't need to rush out the tape recorder every time you come across a good descriptive passage, but your students will find it a welcome and enjoyable change of pace. For grades four through six, John Bellairs's tale of wizardry and an evil sorcerer plotting the end of the world, *The House with a Clock in Its Walls,* includes a mansion filled with every type of clock, including the sinister one from the title. After reading aloud the description of the midnight chimes on pages 15 and 16, have your students recreate the mood and the clamor of all the clocks striking at once.

Several other titles with good "sound" possibilities include Robert McCloskey's *Make Way for Ducklings,* with the combination of traffic and quacking, and the storm scene starting on page 42 of his *A Time of Wonder. Crash! Bang! Boom!* (Doubleday, 1972) and *Gobble, Growl, Grunt* (Doubleday, 1971) by Peter Spier are each filled with an avalanche of noises, all just waiting to be conducted. Studying volcanoes in science? Try *Hill of Fire* by Thomas P. Lewis for an easy-to-read fictional account of the eruption of Mexico's Paricutin in 1943, and then have your students work out how it might have sounded.

Repetitive Dialogue

Children love to help tell a story when there is a refrain to chant. Acting out a tale with much repetitive dialogue is an ice-breaker for even shy children as they don't need to worry about what to say. Lines are repeated often and are easy to recall. While reading aloud or telling stories such as Robert Kalan's *Jump, Frog, Jump,* Lore Segal's *All the Way Home,* or Paul Galdone's retelling of *The Old Woman and Her Pig,* warm up your young thespians by asking them to repeat the refrains with you.

Cumulative sequence stories are a good choice to use with younger children who enjoy the linear structure of cause and effect. When acting out Galdone's *The Old Woman and Her Pig,* I have found that even kindergartners have no trouble remembering and reciting the entire final sequence in which the cat begins to kill the mouse who starts to gnaw the rope that attempts to hang the butcher who starts to kill the ox who commences drinking the water that tries to quench the fire that begins to burn the stick that beats the dog who bites the pig who finally jumps over the stile.

Working in pairs again, enact the confrontation between the two principals in *The Monster and the Tailor* by Paul Galdone, the master illustrator of memorable folktales. As the monster emerges from the grave, urging the frightened tailor to watch, the tailor replies, "I see that, but I'll sew this." Include the final chase scene in which the tailor barely escapes into the castle and the monster leaves his massive handprint on the palace wall.

Exploring Characterization Through Speech

Now that you've considered the possibilities of using narrative pantomime and sound effects with your students, it's valuable to delve a bit deeper into the emotional development of story characters as perceived by children. In order to comprehend why characters behave the ways they do, it is helpful for children to relate their own lives to the fictional ones about which they are reading.

Character Interviews

As an alternative to a general discussion of the whys and wherefores of protagonists and antagonists, conduct an interview with yourself as the host and with your students as subjects and audience. For instance, say you and your sixth graders have just completed the unsettling novel *Is There Life on a Plastic Planet?* by Mildred Ames. Announce to the class that you have somehow managed to induce most of the characters from the book to appear on your talk show and introduce Hollis, the main character, as the first guest. Ask if she's in the room, and as you peer at your audience, either wait for someone to volunteer or say, "Oh, yes, there she is. Hollis, we're so glad you could make it today," and point to one of your more verbal students. You need as a first "guest" that person who is willing to become transformed instantly into a new character, without being self-conscious or tongue-tied.

Once "Hollis" is sitting in a chair next to you, facing the audience, inform your audience that you intend to find out more about that chubby girl who traded her public existence with a life-sized doll twin. Start off the questioning, but tell the audience that they are also welcome to raise their hands and ask questions.

Once the ice is broken, many children will want to volunteer to be interviewed in character. Several students, one after another, can be interviewed as the same character, answering different questions. If a child is reticent, only offering one-word answers, begin with literal questions requiring responses of only a few words. Change characters frequently to give more students a chance to be in the limelight.

The interview technique enables children to develop oral language and creative thinking skills, as they must incorporate knowledge of plot structure, story sequence, setting, and character personalities into their questions and responses. As students will both sympathize and identify with major and minor characters, here is the chance to measure affective or emotional response to a work of literature, in addition to the more straightforward cognitive or factual response.

As you conduct the interviews, keep in mind the different types of questions that can be asked of such diverse personalities as those in *Is There Life on a Plastic Planet?*, including Ms. Eudora, the deceptively sweet doll factory owner; Addison, Hollis's bratty cousin who becomes her only ally; parents, teachers, classmates, and the human-like doll playmates. Innocent bystanders and minor characters make fine subjects for questioning also.

The following list covers various literal, interpretive, critical, and creative questions that you might pose during a class interview of the characters from *Is There Life on a Plastic Planet?* The students in the audience will undoubtedly think up their own questions as well.

Character Being Interviewed	Questions To Ask
Hollis:	How old are you? Why did you hate school? Why did you hate your cousin, Addison? How did you discover Ms. Eudora's Shop of Living Dolls? What did you think of Ms. Eudora when you first met her? What do you think of her now? Why did you want a doll to take your place? What went wrong with your plan? How have you changed since you escaped from Ms. Eudora?
Hollis's Mother:	Do you like your daughter? Have you noticed any changes in her lately? Why did Hollis have to take so many kinds of lessons?
Hollis's Cousin, Addison:	How would you describe yourself? Do you have many friends? Why not? How did you and Hollis become allies? Didn't you once hate each other? Why did you cause so much trouble in school? How did you feel when you discovered your new playmates at Ms. Eudora's were really dolls? How did you escape from being turned into a doll?
Ms. Eudora:	Are you a human or a doll? What is the purpose of your work? Do you think it was right to lure children into your workshop so that you could turn them into dolls? What will you do now?
Hollis's Teacher, Mrs. Broome:	What kind of student has Hollis been this year? What did she get on her last report card?

	Have you noticed any changes in her? Tell us about your newest student, Addison.
Classmates:	Is Hollis a friend of yours? Why or why not? What kind of person is she? What do you think of her cousin, Addison?

Any memorable story with diverse and potentially complex main characters is fair game for the interviewing technique. Fairy tales are a good source; although little detail is given about each character, children will make remarkable inferences about each one. Good choices include P.C. Asbjornsen's *The Squire's Bride,* Pura Belpre's *Oté, Fin M'Coul, the Giant of Knockmany Hill* by Tomie de Paola, *Little Sister and the Month Brothers* by Beatrice Schenk de Regniers, "Rumplestiltskin" or almost any other Grimm tale, and innumerable others.

Using easy fiction, younger children can get into the act as well. Bill Peet's characters are usually worth a closer look. Bernard Waber's "Lyle" books are also full of unusual characters. In *Lyle, Lyle, Crocodile,* aside from the large, friendly reptile of the title, there are the uncomplicated Primm family, unfriendly next-door neighbor Mr. Grumps and his terrified cat Loretta, assorted neighborhood kids, and Hector P. Valenti, star of stage and screen.

The Big Yellow Balloon by Edward Fenton is another obvious choice for narrative pantomime, improvised dialogue, and the interview. In the course of the story, a policeman chases a thief following the old lady who clatters after the dogcatcher who creeps after the dog who patters after the cat who is stalking Roger's big yellow balloon. After assigning the parts, do a narrative pantomime to set the sequence the first time through. Now run through the story again, this time allowing students to improvise their own dialogue to personalize each of the chasers and chased. Afterward, interview the characters to flesh out their various motives and to elicit reaction to the climax, when the cat pops the balloon.

Characters on Trial

Another way to get your students pondering the intricacies of a character's personality is to hold a mock trial. *The Rise and Fall of Ben Gizzard* by Richard Kennedy is an ideal choice for grades three to six. According to an old Indian's prophecy, Ben would die on the day he saw a white mountain upside down and a black bird spoke to him. Mindful of this prediction, he became the villainous sheriff of Depression Gulch, a silver mining town bereft of trees, birds, and mountains, and ultimately met his fate in the form of an innocent young painter.

After a discussion of how your court will operate, appoint counsel for the defense and prosecution of this evil man and permit each side time to discuss the case and develop questions. Lawyers may call main and minor characters as witnesses. Again, questions should require a range of responses, from simple one-word answers to those that entail thought and ingenuity. Your role as the judge is to supervise and add comments or advice as needed.

Two Character Dialogues

You do not always need to witness each dramatic exchange between your students. In many stories, two conflicting characters must resolve a problem, and children can pair up to enact the solution. The purpose of this exercise is for children to argue out a problem where each must listen and respond to the other partner. For younger grades, a good discussion will ensue as Minneapolis Simpkin tries to convince her mother to let her have a pet in Peggy Parish's *No More Monsters for Me*. After the children choose partners, allow them up to five minutes to conduct their arguments and settlements. Then get together to see how each pair ironed out its difficulties.

Third through fifth graders can pair off to become Ellen Toliver and her grandfather who convinces her to take a message through British troops to General Washington. In this exciting historical fiction, *Toliver's Secret* by Esther Wood Brady, Ellen, a meek scaredy-cat, is horrified when her grandfather elects her to undertake the dangerous mission. In another pairs dialogue possibility, Ellen must convince a hungry British soldier not to take her loaf of bread. Ellen is disguised as a boy, and the loaf contains a snuffbox with the secret message. What the soldier considers a mere argument over bread is a matter of urgency for Ellen, who is terrified of being discovered.

Near the end of *Is There Life on a Plastic Planet?*, Hollis meets and argues with the doll that has replaced her. Students can pair up to re-enact and try to resolve that conflict, as the doll claims to be Hollis and will not leave the house.

Improvised Dialogue

Understated or exaggerated humor can pass right over children's heads. They know they're supposed to laugh, but aren't always sure why. After reading aloud *Mr. Yowder and the Train Robbers* by Glen Rounds to a fifth grade class, I wondered if they understood the irony of the ending, so we undertook to act out the last scene.

The story runs as follows: After mild-mannered Mr. Yowder is put down a dry well by outlaws who have interrupted his fishing holiday, he calls upon a rattlesnake acquaintance for help. Then, with the ingenious assistance of several dozen local rattlers, Mr. Yowder plots the capture of the train robbers so that he can gain the reward. Both he and the snakes stake out the abandoned hotel where the crooks return to divide their loot, and before the bad guys know what hit them, they are encircled by the ominously buzzing snakes. Mr. Yowder and company round up all weapons and herd the dismayed captives out to the road. Suddenly, a posse comes galloping toward them, and a smiling Mr. Yowder steps out, holds out his hand for them to stop—and then dives for the ditch as the posse thunders past, the sheriff hollering, "Can't stop now. We're looking for the train robbers! THERE'S A BIG REWARD!"

Naturally, when the dust settles, the snakes have slithered, the crooks have scattered, and Mr. Yowder is back where he started, with nothing to show for his gallant plan.

We set the scene with two children playing Mr. Yowder, six outlaws, twelve snakes and four posse members. We discussed the importance of listening so that everyone would not talk at the same time. By moving furniture, we designated the table in the hotel where the robbers would congregate and the road where all would end up. Each group took a few minutes to plot out the sequence of their movements and the dialogue needed. The snakes practiced their rattling and threatening looks.

The play began. The Misters Yowder had worked out a signal to summon the snakes, and the robbers looked truly

Illustration from THE HOBOKEN CHICKEN EMERGENCY by D. Manus Pinkwater. Copyright © 1977 by D. Manus Pinkwater. Published by Prentice-Hall, Inc., Englewood Cliffs, NJ 07632.

surprised and scared when they found themselves encircled and outnumbered. The actors had no trouble with talking tough and creating believable dialogue, and when the posse thundered in, everyone scattered, leaving the poor Yowders in dismay.

After a good laugh and a discussion of how to improve, we recast those who wanted to change parts and went through the whole scene again. This time, the dialogue was smoother, the snakes were quietly menacing, and there was more tension and fear until the posse arrived. Everyone especially adored diving out of the way of the thundering hooves and would have opted for a third run, if we had had more time.

When we dramatized this story, I made a startling discovery. The fifth grade teacher, upon entering the library and observing her children strutting, rattling, and galloping, shook her head, rolled her eyes, and said, semisarcastically, "Thanks a lot. I'll never get them down to earth now, after all this excitement." And yet, after we finished, the class became noticeably relaxed and calm as they browsed for books. They seemed satisfied and contented with themselves, and not in the least bit rowdy or wound up. After noting the same result with other classes who undertook improvised dramas, I concluded that these activities actually have a calming effect on children, leaving them tired, exhilarated, and feeling very positive about themselves.

To reap the benefits of improvised drama, which for children include increased self-confidence, pride in a job well done, in addition to the usual array of improved comprehension skills, teachers must be willing to allow time for the discussion and planning that come before any actual acting. You must also spend sufficient time on the drama itself, replaying a scene as needed, working out rough spots, and developing characterization. Children will not respond well if you thrust them into an improvised drama without any prior experience to warm them up. Unlike narrative pantomime, which is basically intuitive, improvising dialogue to reconstruct a story or scene is risky for children. They must use reasoning skills, cooperate and interact intimately with their peers, respond to cues, recall a specific sequence, and make the scene become real using their ingenuity. Improvised dialogue is loose and less structured than a scripted play, which stays the same each time.

Some Good Books To Use for Improvised Dialogue

For children in the primary grades, cumulative tales with some improvised dialogue provide a good starting place. "The Travels of a Fox" from Anne Rockwell's *The Old Woman and Her Pig and 10 Other Stories* is a satisfying story, for the sequence is easy to recall, there are enough characters for everyone to have a part, and the dialogue is simple enough to either remember or invent. (Paul Galdone changed the story a bit in *What's in Fox's Sack?*, which is also fun to use.) After casting the fox, the various mistresses of each house, a bumblebee, and all the other assorted animals, have everyone sit in one long row in the order of each character's appearance. Students will have no trouble moving in and out of each scene as needed. You may need to do some side-coaching, or narrating the story line, in between the dialogue. Side-coaching keeps the action flowing smoothly. Use a thick rope or long piece of cloth to simulate the fox's sack, which can be tied loosely around the necks of the successive characters. Sometimes a simple prop will make the story more believable.

Other good cumulative tales include *The Bean Boy* by Joan Chase Bowden, *The Fat Cat* by Jack Kent, and "The Cat and the Parrot" from Virginia Haviland's *Favorite Fairy Tales Told in India*. All three are similar and would be interesting to compare.

Picking choice plums for improvised dialogue from fiction and folklore is an ongoing project with endless capital choices. Even wordless books are prime candidates for acting out, stuffed as they are with slapstick, suspense, and reaction. Look for Mercer Mayer's *Frog Goes to Dinner* (Dial, 1974), John Goodall's *Creepy Castle* (Atheneum, 1975), or Fernando Krahn's *Who's Seen the Scissors?* (Dutton, 1975) just for starters. Devising dialogue where none previously existed is a challenge, for the children will recall the sequence, but will be on their own for what they say.

Folktales often provide enough parts for everyone to jump in. A great example is *Could Anything Be Worse?*, a Jewish folktale retold by Marilyn Hirsch. The poor man of the house can find no peace from his scolding wife and noisy children, so he visits the rabbi for advice. The rabbi tells him to bring first the chickens, then the cow, and finally his freeloading brother and sister-in-law to stay in the house, and the chaos builds. As he reverses the sequence and one by one kicks out each intruder, he finds tranquility at last. Before acting out this tale, discuss with your students the necessity of staying in character so that the play doesn't turn into a free-for-all. It might be wise to bang a hand drum to freeze the action periodically, as the story is noisy, although deliriously funny.

Children are fascinated with the plot and the realistic pencil illustrations in the Caldecott winner *Jumanji* by Chris Van Allsburg. Enhance the story even more by actually playing that dangerous game. Find or make one large die, and ask each student to dream up one new move for the game board, such as, "Caught in a tornado. Lose one turn." Up to four players at a time can compete to reach the golden city of Jumanji, while the rest of the class comprises a human game board, lined up around the room. One at a time, each player rolls and counts off the number of "squares" by touching the hand of each corresponding child in the game board line. When the player lands, the "Square" comes to life, reciting its consequences and acting them out. (The tornado, for instance, would twist and howl.) This activity is great fun, and you may want to go even farther by requesting your students to dream up and design their own games, replete with rules and game board, for others in the class to play.

Since not every story has enough characters to go around, don't be afraid to assign two or more children the same part or to have some children as spectators. Another alternative is to divide the class into groups so that each group can work on a different scene from one or more books.

For *Sir Toby Jingle's Beastly Journey* by Wallace Tripp, three groups can recreate the scenes in which the bear, dragon, and griffin try unsuccessfully to seal up the fierce old knight in a cave, crush him with a tree trunk, and drown him in a well. Another group can show how Sir Toby outwits these creatures, who then become entertainers at his castle.

Using three books the kids know well, assign three skits. For example, fourth and fifth graders can dramatize Billy's encounter with the first worm in Thomas Rockwell's *How To Eat Fried Worms,* the classroom scene in the first chapter of Daniel Pinkwater's *Fat Men from Space,* when Mr. Wendell can't figure out who has the hidden radio, and the kidnapping of Polly and Josh by two strangers who claim to be Polly's aunt and uncle in *Prisoners at the Kitchen Table* by

Barbara Holland. Students will need to ponder—with your help, of course—how to set up each scene and what to say, a good experience in cooperation for everyone.

A Warning from the Author

Don't be surprised when the creative dramatics you try with your students turns out to be wildly successful. It may well end up the high point of your year. It's up to you to figure out what to say after you finish reading a story to your class and your children beg, "May we act it out now?" If your answer is, "Yes," you will not regret it.

If these ideas have whetted your appetite, look for many more suggestions in the annotated book list sections that follow.

Illustration from MR. YOWDER AND THE TRAIN ROBBERS by Glen Rounds. Copyright © 1981 by Glen Rounds. Reproduced by permission of Holiday House.

Introduction to the Read-Aloud Lists

Often the sheer array of titles in the library is enough to give any teacher pause, especially when he or she is looking for a special book to share with students. The read-aloud lists that follow consist (in my own very biased opinion) of many of the best children's books available today. Most of the books have been "kid-tested," i.e., enthusiastically approved by children, who either read the books or heard them read aloud by parents, teachers, or librarians. Not every book will appeal to every teacher, librarian, or child, and you can well afford to be very particular.

Each entry includes the author (or authors), complete title, illustrator, publisher, copyright date, and annotation. If no illustrator is listed, assume either that the author did the art work or, if the book is for older children, that there are no illustrations. Annotations are extremely brief, to give you just an inkling of each book's contents and, where applicable, suggestions for follow-up activities. Lists are overlapping in terms of recommended grade levels (K–1, 1–2, etc.). It is often folly to prescribe an age level to a book, although my aim has been to peg each book to the grades I have found to be most suited to it. Even so, what excites one class or teacher may seem dull or even outrageous to another, depending on levels of interest and maturity. For these reasons, do not feel obligated to stick only to those books on your grade level lists. Moreover, upper grade teachers should not miss using with their students the more sophisticated picture books listed for grades K–3. Older children often appreciate these stories more than the younger children for whom they are intended. It's up to you and your students to decide which material suits the occasion.

Fiction Lists

Almost all the fiction lists include both "Fiction" and "Easy Fiction" titles, as the two categories overlap. What is shelved in the "Easy" section in one library may well be housed in "Fiction" at another. Books on the "Read-Aloud Fiction for Grades K–1" list are exclusively easy fiction and picture books which can be read in one sitting. On the fiction lists for grades 1–2 and 2–3, longer books are noted as such in the annotations, i.e., "Read in installments" or "Read a chapter or two a day" or just "Chapters." Only a few picture books are included in the grades 3–4 and 4–5 lists; titles for grades 5–6 are all longer fiction.

Folk & Fairy Tales, Myths & Legends and Poetry Lists

Folk and fairy tales are divided into two separate sections. The first consists of single, illustrated stories, most of which are best suited to grades K–3, although those tales that appeal to older listeners are marked as such in the annotations. The second section is for folktale collections, in which from three to over three dozen stories are compiled into a single volume. Many of these collections are broad-based in appeal, so each annotation includes the grade level interest span. When you select one of these collections to read aloud, pick only those stories you can't resist and let your students discover the rest.

The authors listed for the books in these two sections are mostly retellers, as no one really knows who originally composed the stories. Translators' names are also included where applicable. In addition, because there are so many fine versions of the German tales collected by Jacob and Wilhelm Grimm, for easy access these titles are all listed under "Grimm, Jacob."

On the poetry list note that "comp.," for compiler, is written after many of the authors' names. This means that the author listed did not write the material, but collected and edited it from various sources.

If you are a teacher and you find, upon checking the card catalog diligently, that your library does not have many of these titles, ask your librarian to consider ordering them. Librarians are delighted to find new books that their readers will love! Unfortunately, with the current state of affairs in the publishing world, some titles will be out of print. If your library does not already own a copy, ordering from a jobber or the publisher will prove futile. You could write to the publisher and complain, but don't count on spectacular results.

When you read the books listed in the pages that follow, you will find yourself amused, astonished, enthralled, tickled, enlightened, and enmeshed in stories which your children will appreciate, all the while clamoring for more. A love of children's literature is contagious, resulting in an epidemic that may well spread to everyone in your school, if you're careful. All schools should encounter and prosper from such an enjoyable disease.

Illustration by Alan Tiegreen from RAMONA QUIMBY, AGE 8 by Beverly Cleary. Copyright © 1981 by Beverly Cleary. Reproduced by permission of William Morrow & Company.

Read-Aloud Fiction
for Grades K–1

Adams, Adrienne. *A Woggle of Witches*. Scribner, 1971.
(Spooky Halloween fare. Students can pantomime witches' flight.)

Aliki. *Keep Your Mouth Closed, Dear*. Dial, 1966.
(Alligator swallows everything, from a clock to the zipper his mother puts on his mouth to cure him.)

——————. *We Are Best Friends*. Greenwillow, 1982.
(Boy left behind when his friend moves. Good discussion starter.)

Allard, Harry. *I Will Not Go to Market Today*. Illus. by James Marshall. Dial, 1979.
(Fenimore B. Buttercrunch, a rooster with bad luck, keeps getting delayed. With editing, a nifty pantomime.)

——————. *It's So Nice To Have a Wolf Around the House*. Illus. by James Marshall. Houghton, 1978.
(Cuthbert Q. Devine proves that even a wolf with a wicked past can reform.)

——————. *The Stupids Step Out*. Illus. by James Marshall. Houghton, 1978.
(Wacky family goes visiting. Also look for other equally silly "Stupid family" books such as *The Stupids Have a Ball*, 1978, and *The Stupids Die*, 1981. Students can make up new "Stupid" stories.)

Allen, Marjorie N. *One, Two, Three—Ah–choo!* Illus. by Dick Gackenbach. Coward, 1980.
(Allergic boy needs a pet that won't make him sneeze.)

Anderson, C.W. *Blaze and the Gray Spotted Pony*. Macmillan, 1968.
(Nice horse tale; one of a series about Billy and his horse, Blaze.)

Anderson, Karen Born. *What's the Matter Sylvie, Can't You Ride?* Dial, 1981.
(Girl masters her new two-wheeler.)

Armitage, Ronda and David. *The Bossing of Josie*. Deutsch, 1980.
(A witch outfit for a birthday present gives Josie the chance to do some of her own bossing.)

Asch, Frank. *Happy Birthday, Moon*. Prentice, 1982.
(Bear exchanges gifts with the moon.)

——————. *Popcorn*. Parents, 1979.
(Bear gets a houseful when he pops too much at his Hal-

loween party. Bring out the popper and make a snack.)

Baer, Edith. *Words Are like Faces.* Illus. by Karen Gundersheimer. Pantheon, 1980.
(Tiny book, lovely poem. Children can decide on their own favorite words.)

Balian, Lorna. *The Aminal.* Abingdon, 1972.
(Patrick finds a round, green, blinky-eyed, pricky-toenailed, waggy-tailed creature.)

————. *Bah! Humbug?* Abingdon, 1977.
(Santa is real!? Little girl and her skeptical brother find out.)

————. *The Sweet Touch.* Abingdon, 1976.
(Genie's spell causes everything Peggy touches to turn into candy.)

Barrett, Judi. *Benjamin's 365 Birthdays.* Illus. by Ron Barrett. Atheneum, 1974.
(Bear finds a way to get gifts all year long.)

Barton, Byron. *Applebet Story.* Viking, 1973.
(Alphabet sequence story. Children can guess the word that goes with each letter.)

Bate, Lucy. *Little Rabbit's Loose Tooth.* Illus. by Diane de Groat. Crown, 1975.
(It falls out, finally.)

Battles, Edith. *The Terrible Trick or Treat.* Illus. by Tom Funk. Scott, 1970.
(Christopher goes out a day early by mistake.)

Bemelmans, Ludwig. *Madeline.* Viking, 1939.
(Classic French rhymed story of a convent school child who gets appendicitis.)

————. *Madeline's Rescue.* Viking, 1953.
(A dog saves her from drowning in the Seine. A Caldecott Award book.)

Bonne, Rose. *I Know an Old Lady.* Illus. by Abner Graboff. Rand, 1961.
(An illustrated version of the song about a ravenous old woman who swallows a fly, spider, bird, cat, dog, goat, and horse before expiring. If you can't sing, chant and your students will join in on the sequence.)

Bonsall, Crosby. *Tell Me Some More.* Illus. by Fritz Siebel. Harper, 1961.
(The magic of books and libraries. Set aside books on lions, camels, rockets, giraffes, and elephants and show as they come up in the story.)

Bottner, Barbara. *Messy.* Delacorte, 1979.

(Sloppy girl tries to reform.)

Bozzo, Maxine. *Toby in the Country, Toby in the City*. Illus. by Frank Modell. Greenwillow, 1982.
(Two children show the differences between their environments. Fine for social studies discussion.)

Brandenberg, Franz. *I Wish I Was Sick, Too!* Illus. by Aliki. Greenwillow, 1976.
(Cat sister is jealous of her brother's illness until she catches it.)

—————. *No School Today*. Illus. by Aliki. Macmillan, 1975.
(Cat brother and sister get up too early.)

Brenner, Barbara. *Mr. Tall and Mr. Small*. Illus. by Tomi Ungerer. Young Scott, 1966.
(What's better—tall or small? A giraffe and his mouse friend can't agree.)

Brown, Marc Tolon. *Arthur's Eyes*. Little, Brown, 1979.
(Aardvark needs glasses.)

Brown, Marcia. *How, Hippo!* Scribner, 1969.
(Little Hippo is caught unawares by a crocodile.)

Brown, Margaret Wise. *The Runaway Bunny*. Illus. by Clement Hurd. Harper, 1972.
(How a loving rabbit mother talks her rebellious son into staying home.)

—————. *The Steamroller*. Illus. by Evaline Ness. Walker, 1974.
(Little girl's Christmas present squashes everything and everybody flat. Great to act out.)

Burningham, John. *Would You Rather. . . .* Crowell, 1978.
(Hilarious big book of unsavory choices. Let children make up their own.)

Burton, Virginia Lee. *Katy and the Big Snow*. Houghton, 1943.
(Tractor plows out town. Good for a snowy day or a social studies lesson on communities.)

—————. *Mike Mulligan and His Steam Shovel*. Houghton, 1939.
(Together they dig the new Town Hall cellar in only one day. Follow up with Sauer's *Mike's House*.)

Carlson, Natalie Savage. *Marie Louise and Christophe at the Carnival*. Illus. by Jose Aruego and Ariane Dewey. Scribner, 1981.
(Mongoose and snake share an adventure. Make your own cat masks afterward.)

——————. *Runaway Marie Louise.* Illus. by Jose Aruego
and Ariane Dewey. Scribner, 1977.
(Mongoose feels unloved after her mama gives her a
spanking.)
——————. *Spooky Night.* Illus. by Andrew Glass. Lothrop,
1982.
(Spooky, a black, pussyfooting witch's cat, must capture
the moon on Halloween before he is allowed to go back to
his human family.)
Cazet, Denys. *Lucky Me.* Macmillan, 1983.
(Cumulative tale of a chicken being followed by a fox and
other animals, all looking for a free meal. Clever to act out
with improvised dialogue.)
Christelow, Eileen. *Henry and the Red Stripes.* Clarion,
1982.
(Rabbit's hand-painted stripes save him from a hungry fox
family.)
——————. *Mr. Murphy's Marvelous Invention.* Clarion,
1983.
(Pig's new housework machine misdoes all the chores.)
Cleveland, David. *The April Rabbits.* Illus. by Nurit Karlin.
Coward, 1978.
(Hilarious for April Fools' Day and narrative pantomime
with children being the rabbits.)
Cohen, Miriam. *Lost in the Museum.* Illus. by Lillian Hoban.
Greenwillow, 1979.
(Read before your next class trip!)
——————. *No Good in Art.* Illus. by Lillian Hoban. Green-
willow, 1980.
(First grade boy lacks confidence in his drawing abilities.)
Cole, Brock. *No More Baths.* Doubleday, 1980.
(Dirty little girl runs away. Fun to act out as you read.)
Cole, Joanna. *Golly Gump Swallowed a Fly.* Illus. by Bari
Weissman. Dutton, 1982.
(New prose variant of the song "I Know an Old Lady Who
Swallowed a Fly." Fun to tell.)
Cooney, Nancy Evans. *The Blanket That Had To Go.* Illus. by
Diane Dawson. Putnam, 1981.
(Susi dreads leaving her blanket behind when kindergar-
ten starts.)
——————. *The Wobbly Tooth.* Illus. by Marilyn Hafner. Put-
nam, 1978.
(Elizabeth's loose tooth refuses to come out.)
Craig, M. Jean. *The Dragon in the Clock Box.* Illus. by Kelly
Oechsli. Norton, 1962.

Illustration from THE STORIES JULIAN TELLS by Ann Cameron. Text copyright © 1981 by Ann Cameron. Illustrations copyright © 1981 by Ann Strugnell. Published by Pantheon Books, a division of Random House, Inc.

(Boy's imaginary dragon hatches. Hand out invisible dragon eggs for your children to hatch and have them write about and draw them.)

Cressey, James. *Fourteen Rats & a Rat-Catcher*. Illus. by Tamasin Cole. Prentice, 1977.

(Old lady versus the rats in her basement. Fun to act out.)

Degen, Bruce. *Jamberry*. Harper, 1983.

(Berryland jam pickers on an unforgettable rhyming jam jamboree. It's the berries!)

Delton, Judy. *Two Good Friends*. Illus. by Giulio Maestro. Crown, 1974.

(Messy bear bakes while neat duck cleans.)

De Regniers, Beatrice Schenk. *May I Bring a Friend?* Illus. by Beni Montresor. Atheneum, 1964.

(Boy visits king and queen with his zoo pals. A Caldecott Medal winner.)

Dillon, Barbara. *The Beast in the Bed*. Illus. by Chris Conover. Morrow, 1981.

(Small green beast is a companion to lonely children until they reach school age.)

Douglass, Barbara. *Good as New*. Illus. by Patience Brewster. Lothrop, 1982.

(Grandpa fixes up Grady's damaged stuffed bear. A good companion to Don Freeman's *Corduroy*. Have a bear party in your room.)

DuVoisin, Roger. *Petunia*. Knopf, 1950.

(Silly goose finds a book which she thinks will make her wise.)

Emberley, Ed. *The Wing on a Flea*. Little, Brown, 1961.

(Rhyming book about shapes.)

Ets, Marie Hall. *Talking Without Words*. Viking, 1968.

(Non-verbal communication. Children can pantomime each emotion presented.)

Fatio, Louise. *The Happy Lion*. Illus. by Roger DuVoisin. McGraw-Hill, 1954.

(French zoo lion gets out for a stroll around town.)

Felt, Sue. *Rosa-Too-Little*. Doubleday, 1950.

(Rosa can't have her own library card until she can print her name.)

Fenner, Carol. *Tigers in the Cellar*. Harcourt, 1963.

("Rumbly, tumbly, pull my toes . . .," they sing to the little girl who believes in them.)

Flack, Marjorie. *Angus and the Cat*. Doubleday, 1931.

(Curious Scotty dog meets feline.)

————. *Angus and the Ducks*. Doubleday, 1930.

(Scotty dog loses his curiosity.)

————. *Angus Lost*. Doubleday, 1932.

(Scotty dog gets out of his yard. Make a sound effects tape with your students of the book's many noises.)

————. *Ask Mr. Bear*. Macmillan, 1932.

(Animals advise boy on his mother's birthday present. Classes love to act this out.)

————. *The Story About Ping*. Viking, 1933.

(Duckling on the Yangtze River.)

Freeman, Don. *Bearymore*. Viking, 1976.

(Circus bear needs a new act to keep his job.)

————. *Corduroy*. Viking, 1968.

(Stuffed bear searches for his lost button. Also read the 1978 sequel *A Pocket for Corduroy*.)

————. *Dandelion*. Viking, 1964.

(Lion gussies up for a party. Good discussion starter on being yourself.)

————. *Hattie the Backstage Bat*. Viking, 1970.

(Thanks to a theater bat with a sense of timing, the new mystery play is a hit.)

————. *Mop Top*. Viking, 1955.

(Sent by his mother to the barber, Moppy hides in the grocery store instead.)

————. *Quiet! There's a Canary in the Library*. Golden Gate, 1969.

(Little girl imagines all the animals she would invite to the library. Assign parts and act out with all appropriate sound effects.)

Gackenbach, Dick. *Harry and the Terrible Whatzit,* Seabury, 1977.

(There's a monster lurking in the cellar, and Harry gets rid of it.)

Gaeddert, Lou Ann. *Noisy Nancy Norris*. Illus. by Gioia Fiammenghi. Doubleday, 1965.

(Downstairs apartment owner, Mrs. Muffle, insists on complete peace and quiet from Nancy, a rambunctious and buoyant little girl.)

Gag, Wanda. *The Funny Thing*. Coward, 1929.

(A doll-eating dragon reforms.)

————. *Millions of Cats*. Coward, 1928.

(Classic of an old man who couldn't pick just one. Children love to chant refrain.)

Gage, Wilson. *Cully Cully and the Bear*. Illus. by James Stevenson. Greenwillow, 1983.

(A confused old codger and an angry bear chase each other around and around a tree. Would make a hilarious pairs pantomime, although you'll need lots of space—outside, perhaps—for each pair to run around its own imaginary tree.)

Gantos, Jack. *Greedy Greeny*. Illus. by Nicole Rubel. Doubleday, 1979.
(Monster has a nightmare caused by guilt and overeating. Fun to act out. Serve a watermelon treat.)

——————. *Rotten Ralph*. Illus. by Nicole Rubel. Houghton, 1976.
(Red cat will not behave. Have students pantomime cat's naughtiness as you read.)

Getz, Arthur. *Humphrey the Dancing Pig*. Dial, 1980.
(Pig thins down like the cat. Children of all ages love to pantomime the various dances Humphrey tries.)

Ginsburg, Mirra. *The Chick and the Duckling*. Illus. by Jose and Ariane Aruego. Macmillan, 1972.
(Simple tale for children to act out in pairs.)

——————. *Mushroom in the Rain*. Illus. by Jose Aruego and Ariane Dewey. Macmillan, 1974.
(Animals hide from weather and hungry fox. Fun to act out as a group using improvised dialogue.)

Graham, Margaret Bloy. *Benjy and the Barking Bird*. Harper, 1971.
(Jealous dog versus a smart-mouthed parrot.)

Gramatky, Hardie. *Hercules*. Putnam, 1940.
("The story of an old-fashioned fire engine." A classic.)

Green, Norma B. *The Hole in the Dike*. Illus. by Eric Carle. Crowell, 1974.
(Famous story of a brave Dutch boy.)

Himmelman, John. *Talester the Lizard*. Dial, 1982.
(Lizard befriends his own reflection. Pair up for a mirror pantomime.)

Hoban, Lillian. *Arthur's Christmas Cookies*. Harper, 1972.
(Chimp botches up the recipe. Good lead-in to crafts or cooking activity.)

Hoban, Russell. *A Baby Sister for Frances*. Illus. by Lillian Hoban. Harper, 1964.
(Badger feels unloved with the new baby in the house.)

——————. *Bedtime for Frances*. Illus. by Garth Williams. Harper, 1960.
(Badger is simply not sleepy.)

——————. *Best Friends for Frances*. Illus. by Lillian Hoban. Harper, 1969.

(Little sisters come in handy sometimes.)

————. *Bread and Jam for Frances*. Illus. by Lillian Hoban. Harper, 1964.

(Frances won't try any new foods, so her mother gives her bread and jam for every meal. Read in tandem with Bruce Degen's *Jamberry*, then make jam sandwiches with your class. Also similar in theme to Mary Rayner's *Mrs. Pig's Bulk Buy*.)

Hoban, Tana. *Push, Pull; Empty, Full*. Macmillan, 1972.

(Photographed book of opposites.)

Hoff, Syd. *Lengthy*. Putnam, 1964.

(Dog makes dachshunds look short in comparison. Have class come up with new ways he could be useful.)

Hughes, Shirley. *Alfie Gets in First*. Lothrop, 1981.

(Little boy accidentally locks his mother out of the house.)

————. *David and Dog*. Prentice, 1977.

(Boy loses his favorite stuffed animal.)

————. *Moving Molly*. Prentice, 1979.

(Little girl moves to a new house and finds a secret place.)

Hutchins, Pat. *Rosie's Walk*. Macmillan, 1968.

(Hen inadvertently escapes fox's trail each time in this amusing wordless sequence story. Good for retelling by students and for pairs pantomime, with the action narrated by you.)

Isadora, Rachel. *Max*. Macmillan, 1976.

(On the way to his baseball game, Max warms up at his sister's ballet class. Lead your young dancers in some leaps and bends.)

Jeschke, Susan. *Angela and Bear*. Holt, 1979.

(Angela's new magic crayons cause her polar bear drawing to come to life.)

Johnson, Crockett. *Harold and the Purple Crayon*. Harper, 1955.

(Wonderful drawing story for children to act out or draw adventures with their own "magic" purple crayons.)

————. *Will Spring Be Early? or Will Spring Be Late?* Crowell, 1959.

(Stray plastic flower causes groundhog to predict spring's arrival in February.)

Johnston, Johanna. *Edie Changes Her Mind*. Illus. by Paul Galdone. Putnam, 1964.

(Little girl who hates bedtime is allowed to stay up all night.)

Johnston, Tony. *Mole and Troll Trim the Tree*. Illus. by Wallace Tripp. Putnam, 1974.

(Two best friends fight over the correct way to decorate the Christmas tree. Amusing prelude to decorating the classroom tree.)

Kalan, Robert. *Jump, Frog, Jump.* Illus. by Byron Barton. Greenwillow, 1981.

(Sequence story of a frog's narrow escapes. Students will chant refrain.)

Keats, Ezra Jack. *Dreams.* Macmillan, 1974.

(Roberto can't sleep. A thoughtful and beautiful discussion starter.)

——————. *Goggles!* Macmillan, 1969.

(Peter and his friend outwit the big boys with the help of Peter's dog, Willie.)

——————. *Jennie's Hat.* Harper, 1966.

(The birds help her decorate it. Bring in a large straw hat and let your students create the finery.)

——————. *A Letter to Amy.* Harper, 1968.

(Peter worries that his friend Amy won't come to his party. Practice writing your own invitations to a classroom event.)

——————. *Peter's Chair.* Harper, 1967.

(A new baby sister makes him jealous and possessive.)

——————. *The Snowy Day.* Viking, 1962.

(Classic winter story, perfect for sharing and acting out in pantomime. A Caldecott Award winner.)

——————. *Whistle for Willie.* Viking, 1964.

(Peter yearns to be able to whistle so that he can summon his dachshund Willie.)

Kent, Jack. *The Fat Cat.* Parents, 1971.

(Cumulative tale of greedy cat, perfect for acting out.)

——————. *Little Peep.* Prentice, 1981.

(Chick challenges rooster to crow up the sun.)

Kepes, Juliet. *Run, Little Monkeys! Run, Run, Run!* Pantheon, 1974.

(Animals chase them. Class can chant the refrain.)

Kraus, Robert. *Leo the Late Bloomer.* Illus. by Jose Aruego. Windmill, 1971.

(Tiger can't do anything right. For all ages.)

——————. *Milton the Early Riser.* Illus. by Jose and Ariane Aruego. Windmill, 1972.

(Panda can't sleep. Fun to act out as narrative pantomime.)

Kroll, Steven. *The Candy Witch.* Illus. by Marilyn Hafner. Holiday, 1979.

(Girl witch causes mischief on Halloween to attract attention.)

Lasker, Joe. *The Do-Something Day*. Viking, 1982.
(Benjie decides to run away when no one at home has time for him.)

Leaf, Munro. *The Story of Ferdinand*. Illus. by Robert Lawson. Viking, 1936.
(Peaceful bull won't fight. Fine for all ages.)

LeSieg, Theo. *I Wish That I Had Duck Feet*. Random, 1965.
(Boy imagines what it would be like. Have children make illustrations of how they'd like to change if they could.)

Lester, Helen. *Cora Copycat*. Dutton, 1979.
(A wild, wooly wurgal cures girl of her mimicking ways.)

Le-Tan, Pierre. *Happy Birthday, Oliver*. Random, 1979.
(Dog worries that no one has remembered it.)

Leverich, Kathleen. *The Hungry Fox and the Foxy Duck*. Illus. by Paul Galdone. Parents, 1978.
(Fox plans on a duck dinner, but the duck is too clever for him.)

Lexau, Joan. *That's Good, That's Bad*. Illus. by Aliki. Dial, 1963.
(Sequence story of a boy being chased by an angry rhino. Fine to retell and act out.)

Leydenfrost, Robert. *The Snake That Sneezed*. Putnam, 1970.
(Snake bites off more than he can chew. Fun to act out; as each "animal" is swallowed, actors can line up behind the child playing the snake.)

Lindgren, Astrid. *I Want a Brother or Sister*. Illus. by Ilon Wikland. Harcourt, 1978.
(Boy is jealous of new baby sister until he starts to help care for her.)

Lionni, Leo. *Fish Is Fish*. Pantheon, 1970.
(Fish learns about the world through his frog friend's eyes.)

—————. *Inch by Inch*. Obolensky, 1960.
(Inchworm measures birds. Follow up with a measuring activity.)

—————. *Little Blue and Little Yellow*. Obolensky, 1959.
(Blue + yellow = green. A scrap paper story of friendship. Children can invent adventures using torn paper. Also a good time to mix colors and make new ones.)

—————. *Swimmy*. Pantheon, 1963.
(Underwater survival story of little fishes who band together

to thwart a big one.)

Lobel, Anita. *On Market Street*. Greenwillow, 1981.
(An ABC of people made up of apples, books, clocks and so on. If used with older children, they can design their own letter pictures.)

Lobel, Arnold. *Days with Frog and Toad*. Harper, 1979.

――――――. *Frog and Toad All Year*. Harper, 1976.

――――――. *Frog and Toad Are Friends*. Harper, 1970.

――――――. *Frog and Toad Together*. Harper, 1972.
(Frog and Toad books are collections of short, delightful tales of two best friends.)

――――――. *The Great Blueness and Other Predicaments*. Harper, 1968.
(How colors came to be. Break out the paints and start mixing.)

――――――. *How the Rooster Saved the Day*. Illus. by Anita Lobel. Greenwillow, 1977.
(A fast-thinking rooster tricks a thief into calling up the sun.)

――――――. *Mouse Tales*. Harper, 1972.
(Papa Mouse tells seven bedtime stories to his seven children. Try acting out "The Journey" for some giggles.)

MacGregor, Ellen. *Theodore Turtle*. Illus. by Paul Galdone. McGraw, 1955.
(Turtle's absent-mindedness causes him trouble.)

Maestro, Betsy and Giulio, *Lambs for Dinner*. Crown, 1978.
(A friend-seeking wolf invites four suspicious lamb children to his place for supper.)

――――――. *A Wise Monkey Tale*. Crown, 1975.
(Monkey tricks her way out of a hole.)

Marshall, James. *George and Martha*. Houghton, 1972.

――――――. *George and Martha Encore*. Houghton, 1973.

――――――. *George and Martha One Fine Day*. Houghton, 1978.

――――――. *George and Martha Rise and Shine*. Houghton, 1976.

――――――. *George and Martha Tons of Fun*. Houghton, 1980.
(George and Martha books are funny, short vignettes, averaging five per book, of two hippo friends.)

Marshall, James. *The Guest*. Houghton, 1975.
(Moose and snail become best friends.)

Mayer, Mercer. *Professor Wormbog in Search for the Zipperump-a-Zoo*. Golden, 1976.

(The only missing beastie in the professor's collection continues to elude him.)

————. *There's a Nightmare in My Closet*. Dial, 1968.
(Boy overcomes his fear and tames a bedtime monster.)

————. *What Do You Do with a Kangaroo?* Four Winds, 1973.
(Little girl copes with an animal invasion.)

McCloskey, Robert. *Blueberries for Sal*. Viking, 1948.
(A little girl and a bear cub cross paths while out berrying with their mothers.)

McPhail, David. *The Bear's Toothache*. Little, 1972.
(Boy helps bear pull out tooth. Wonderfully understated; try a pairs pantomime.)

————. *Pig Pig Grows Up*. Dutton, 1980.
(Pig Pig enjoys being babied until he sees the advantage of acting his age.)

Meddaugh, Susan. *Beast*. Houghton, 1981.
(Anna finds that the feared beast in the family barn is really rather shy.)

Mendoza, George. *The Sesame Street Book of Opposites*. Platt, 1974.
(Zany full-color photos of a diapered Zero Mostel.)

Mooser, Stephen. *The Ghost with the Halloween Hiccups*. Illus. by Tomie de Paola. Watts, 1977.
(Everyone tries to help Mr. Penny cure his hiccups. Listeners can provide the hic-sound hic-effects.)

Moskin, Marietta D. *Rosie's Birthday Present*. Illus. by David S. Rose. Atheneum, 1981.
(Rosie trades treasures to get the perfect present for her mother.)

Murphy, Jill. *Peace at Last*. Dial, 1980.
(Mr. Bear can't sleep. A perfect story to act out, retell and/or join in on sound effects and refrain.)

Myers, Bernice. *Not This Bear!* Four Winds, 1967.
(Dressed in a fur jacket, Herman is mistaken for a bear and escorted back to the den.)

Palmer, Helen. *A Fish out of Water*. Illus. by P.D. Eastman. Random, 1961.
(Overfed fish *grows*.)

Panek, Dennis. *Catastrophe Cat*. Bradbury, 1978.
(Almost wordless action-filled tale of crazy cat's misadventures; fun for narrative pantomime. Also see *Catastrophe Cat at the Zoo*, 1979.)

Parish, Peggy. *No More Monsters for Me*. Illus. by Marc Simont. Harper, 1981.

(When her mother says, "No pets!" Minn finds a monster instead.)

Parker, Nancy Winslow. *Love from Uncle Clyde.* Dodd, 1977.
(He sends a crated hippo to Charlie. Read without showing any illustrations so that children can draw or describe what they think the present is.)

Payne, Emmy. *Katy No-Pocket.* Illus. by H.A. Rey. Houghton, 1944.
(Pouchless kangaroo searches for a suitable pocket.)

Peet, Bill. *The Ant and the Elephant.* Houghton, 1972.
(After an elephant rescues a stranded ant, the ant returns the favor, proving that even the smallest creatures can be helpful.)

Pinkwater, Daniel M. *The Wuggie Norple Story.* Illus. by Tomie de Paola. Four Winds, 1980.
(Cat keeps growing. Have fun making up new names to go with absurd characters like Lunchbox Louie, Bigfoot the Chipmunk, and Freckleface Chilibean.)

Pinkwater, Manus. *Three Big Hogs.* Seabury, 1975.
(Porkers look for a new home.)

Polushkin, Maria. *Bubba and Babba.* Illus. by Diane de Groat. Crown, 1976.
(Two lazy bears compete for the last word. Based on a Russian folktale.)

—————. *Mother, Mother, I Want Another.* Illus. by Diane Dawson. Crown, 1978.
(Baby mouse just wants another goodnight kiss, but his mother thinks he wants another mother.)

Pomerantz, Charlotte. *Buffy and Albert.* Illus. by Yossi Abolafia. Greenwillow, 1982.
(After Grandpa sprains his ankle, he comes to appreciate the companionship of his two aging bothersome cats.)

—————. *The Piggy in the Puddle.* Illus. by James Marshall. Macmillan, 1974.
(Delicious oofy-poofy nonsense rhyme of a dirty pig and her worried family.)

Potter, Beatrix. *The Tale of Benjamin Bunny.* Warne, n.d.
(Bad rabbit learns his lesson.)

—————. *The Tale of Peter Rabbit.* Warne, n.d.
(The classic tale of the naughty rabbit trapped in Mr. McGregor's garden.)

Preston, Edna Mitchell. *Where Did My Mother Go?* Illus. by Chris Conover. Four Winds, 1978.
(Kitten searches everywhere. Children can join in on the refrain.)

Radin, Ruth Yaffe. *A Winter Place*. Illus. by Mattie Lou O'Kelley. Little, 1982.
(On a winter day, children go into the hills to ice skate. Luminous primitive paintings evoke an American era passed.)

Rey, H.A. *Curious George*. Houghton, 1941.
──────. *Curious George Takes a Job*. Houghton, 1947.
(Children love this everlastingly trouble-making monkey. Introduce them to the other titles in the series as well.)

Robison, Deborah. *No Elephants Allowed*. Houghton, 1981.
(Justin tries to chase elephants out of his room so that he can sleep. At the end, have students guess what he hung on his wall to scare them off.)

Roche, P.K. *Good-bye, Arnold*. Dial, 1979.
(Mouse finds the lack of sibling rivalry is both a pleasure and a bore when his brother goes away for a week.)

Rockwell, Anne. *The Gollywhopper Egg*. Macmillan, 1974.
(Peddler sells coconut to gullible farmer. Bring in a real coconut to crack and eat.)

Roy, Ron. *Three Ducks Went Wandering*. Illus. by Paul Galdone. Seabury, 1979.
(Ducks inadvertently avoid danger in this clever sequence story.)

Sauer, Julia Lina. *Mike's House*. Illus. by Don Freeman. Viking, 1954.
(Boy considers the main character from *Mike Mulligan and His Steam Shovel* to be his best friend. Read in tandem with the Virginia Lee Burton classic.)

Schatell, Brian. *Farmer Goff and His Turkey Sam*. Harper, 1982.
(Pie-loving prize turkey. Fun for November.)

Segal, Lore. *All the Way Home*. Illus. by James Marshall. Farrar, 1973.
(A cumulative crying, barking, meowing, squawking, and grinning story, great for class participation, retelling, and acting out.)

Sendak, Maurice. *Alligators All Around*. Harper, 1962
(Reptilian alphabet book, made for narrative pantomime. Carol King's splendid musical sound track record for the movie *Really Rosie* includes this and the next two titles.)
──────. *Chicken Soup with Rice*. Harper, 1962.
(Monthly rhymes for children to chant.)
──────. *Pierre*. Harper, 1962.
(Indifferent boy only says, "I don't care.")
──────. *Where the Wild Things Are*. Harper, 1963.

(World's best monster tale; students will need to don their imaginary wolf suits beforehand and join in on all the monster noises. A Caldecott Award winner.)

Seuss, Dr. *The Cat in the Hat*. Random, 1957.
(When the cat visits, trouble follows. A deserved favorite.)
──────. *Dr. Seuss' ABC*. Random, 1963.
(From Aunt Annie's alligator to a Zizzer-zazzer-zuzz. Students will dream up more.)
──────. *Marvin K. Mooney, Will You Please Go Now!* Random, 1972.
(Suggesting unusual ways for him to LEAVE. Allow children to invent their own transportation for him.)

Shannon, George. *Dance Away*. Illus. by Jose Aruego and Ariane Dewey. Greenwillow, 1982.
(Rabbit saves friends from fox. Great to act out with dance and chant.)
──────. *Lizard's Song*. Illus. by Jose Aruego and Ariane Dewey. Greenwillow, 1981.
(Bear wants Lizard's song. Act out this one—music is included, and the "Zoli Zoli Zoli" refrain is positively addicting.)

Slobodkin, Florence. *Too Many Mittens*. Hale, 1963.
(Twins lose one red mitten, but end up with many.)

Slobodkina, Esphyr. *Caps for Sale*. W.R. Scott, 1947.
(Monkeys tease peddler. Divide class so that one half play the monkeys and the other half are peddlers. Act out and then switch parts.)

Spier, Peter. *Oh, Were They Ever Happy!* Doubleday, 1978.
(Children take it upon themselves to paint their house rainbow-style.)

Springstubb, Tricia. *The Magic Guinea Pig*. Illus. by Bari Weissman. Morrow, 1982.
(Bumbling witch gives Mark an unexpected pet.)

Stevenson, James. *Clams Can't Sing*. Greenwillow, 1980.
(Oh, yes they can! Make a sound tape of your own beach concert.)
──────. *Monty*. Greenwillow, 1979.
(Patient alligator ferries animals across the water until they take him for granted once too often.)

Sumiko. *Kittymouse*. Harcourt, 1979.
(Kitten is raised by a mouse family.)

Taylor, Mark. *Henry the Explorer*. Illus. by Graham Booth. Atheneum, 1966.
(Boy and Scotty dog discover a cave, get lost, and find their way home.)

Thayer, Jane. *The Popcorn Dragon*. Morrow, 1953.
(Lonely dragon learns to put his fire to good use.)
——————. *Quiet on Account of Dinosaur*. Illus. by Seymour Fleischman. Morrow, 1964.
(Little girl finds a brontosaurus and takes him to school.)
Tresselt, Alvin. *White Snow, Bright Snow*. Illus. by Roger DuVoisin. Lothrop, 1947.
(A Caldecott winner, good for sharing snowy day experiences.)
Turkle, Brinton. *Deep in the Forest*. Dutton, 1976.
(Wordless switch on "The Three Bears." Try both and compare.)
Tworkov, Jack. *The Camel Who Took a Walk*. Illus. by Roger DuVoisin. Aladdin, 1951.
(A jungle sequence story, fun to retell.)
Udry, Janice May. *Alfred*. Illus. by Judith Shuman Roth. Whitman, 1960.
(Young Henry is terrified of all the dogs on his block until the day the biggest one of all, an Irish setter, takes drastic measures to make friends.)
——————. *Thump and Plunk*. Illus. by Ann Schweninger. Harper, 1981.
(Mother mouse wants Thump to stop plunking Plunk's plunkit, and vice versa. A real tongue twister.)
——————. *A Tree Is Nice*. Illus. by Marc Simont. Harper, 1956.
(Gives reasons. A good story starter and a Caldecott winner.)
——————. *What Mary Jo Shared*. Illus. by Eleanor Mill. Whitman, 1966.
(A shy little girl thinks of the perfect thing to share for show-and-tell: her own father.)
Viorst, Judith. *I'll Fix Anthony*. Illus. by Arnold Lobel. Harper, 1969.
(Younger brother plots revenge—as soon as he turns six, that is.)
Vreeken, Elizabeth. *The Boy Who Would Not Say His Name*. Illus. by Leonard Shortall. Follett, 1959.
(Boy pretends to be assorted story characters.)
Waber, Bernard. *The House on East 88th Street*. Houghton, 1962.
(How Lyle the Crocodile came to live at the above New York City address. First in a series.)
——————. *Lyle, Lyle, Crocodile*. Houghton, 1965.
(More adventures of the crocodile from New York City.)

——————. *Rich Cat, Poor Cat*. Houghton, 1963.
(The lives of pampered pets are contrasted with the life of a stray.)

——————. *You Look Ridiculous Said the Rhinocerous to the Hippopotamus*. Houghton, 1966.
(Hippo hates her looks. Would make a wonderful flannel board story.)

Wahl, Jan. *Doctor Rabbit's Foundling*. Illus. by Cyndy Szekeres. Pantheon, 1977.
(Doctor raises Tiny from tadpole to toad.)

Watson, Pauline. *Wriggles, the Little Wishing Pig*. Illus. by Paul Galdone. Seabury, 1978.
(Pig envies other animals until his wishes come true.)

Weiss, Nicki. *Hank and Oogie*. Greenwillow, 1982.
(What a hard time Hank has, giving up his dependence on Oogie, his green stuffed hippo.)

Wells, Rosemary. *Good Night, Fred*. Dial, 1981.
(Little boy's Grandma pops out of the telephone to keep him company.)

——————. *Morris' Disappearing Bag*. Dial, 1975.
(Youngest bear gets the best Christmas present, much to the envy of the older ones.)

——————. *Timothy Goes to School*. Dial, 1981.
(Raccoon is ready to quit until he makes a new friend.)

Whitney, Alma Marshak. *Just Awful*. Illus. by Lillian Hoban. Addison, 1971.
(Boy is afraid to go to the school nurse until his first visit.)

——————. *Leave Herbert Alone*. Illus. by David McPhail. Addison, 1972.
(Jennifer wants the next door cat to like her. Good for pairs pantomime.)

Willoughby, Elaine. *Boris and the Monsters*. Illus. by Lynn Munsinger. Houghton, 1980.
(Little boy is afraid of the dark until he gets a puppy.)

Winthrop, Elizabeth. *Sloppy Kisses*. Illus. by Anne Burgess. Macmillan, 1980.
(Pig thinks she's too old for her parents to kiss her.)

Wittman, Sally. *The Wonderful Mrs. Trumbly*. Illus. by Margot Apple. Harper, 1982.
(Martin is crushed when he discovers that his beloved teacher has a boyfriend.)

Wright, Dare. *The Lonely Doll*. Doubleday, 1957.
(Photo story of Edith the doll and her new teddy bear friends.)

Zion, Gene. *Harry by the Sea*. Illus. by Margaret Bloy Graham. Harper, 1965.

(Family's pet dog causes an uproar at the beach.)

—————. *Harry the Dirty Dog.* Illus. by Margaret Bloy Graham. Harper, 1956.

(Dog gets so dirty, even his own family doesn't recognize him.)

—————. *No Roses for Harry.* Illus. by Margaret Bloy Graham. Harper, 1958.

(Dog hates his new sweater and sets out to lose it.)

Zolotow, Charlotte. *Mr. Rabbit and the Lovely Present.* Illus. by Maurice Sendak. Harper, 1962.

(Girl looks for the perfect present for her mother. As a follow-up, make fruit salad.)

—————. *William's Doll.* Illus. by William Pène du Bois. Harper, 1972.

(Boy wants a doll, much to his parents' chagrin.)

Read-Aloud Fiction
for Grades 1–2

Alexander, Sue. *Marc the Magnificent.* Illus. by Tomie de Paola. Pantheon, 1978.
(Boy magician. Afterward, children can use magic books to practice some tricks.)

Allard, Harry. *Miss Nelson Is Back.* Illus. by James Marshall. Houghton, 1982.
(The students in room 207 object to their substitute teachers. Sequel to *Miss Nelson Is Missing.*)

—————. *Miss Nelson Is Missing.* Illus. by James Marshall. Houghton, 1977.
(How to get your class of misbehavers in line. Great for any grade.)

Allen, Marjorie. *Farley, Are You for Real?* Illus. by Joel Schick. Coward, 1976.
(Boy meets a modern-day genie. Children can compile their own three wishes.)

Ambrus, Victor. *Grandma, Felix and Mustapha Biscuit.* Morrow, 1982.
(A greedy, scheming cat is foiled by the hamster and parrot he wants to eat.)

Amoss, Berthe. *The Great Sea Monster: or, A Book by You.* Parents, 1975.
(How to make a book. Good writing incentive.)

Anderson, C. W. *Blaze and the Forest Fire.* Macmillan, 1938.
(Nice horse story to use during Fire Prevention Week.)

Anderson, Leone Castell. *The Wonderful Shrinking Shirt.* Illus. by Irene Trivas. Whitman, 1983.
(Elbert's fine yellow flannel shirt with purple stripes is passed down each time it is washed to a smaller family member. Have class say the refrain in character each time.)

Anderson, Lonzo. *The Halloween Party.* Illus. by Adrienne Adams. Scribner, 1974.
(Faraday Folsum happens upon a forest party for witches, gremlins, and ogres.)

—————. *Mr. Biddle and the Birds.* Illus. by Adrienne Adams. Scribner, 1971.
(Man flies in a chair-in-the-air with the help of his bird friends.)

—————. *Two Hundred Rabbits.* Illus. by Adrienne Adams. Viking, 1968.

(A poor peasant boy looks for a novel way to entertain the king at the castle festival.)

Annett, Cora. *The Dog Who Thought He Was a Boy*. Houghton, 1965.

(Smart mutt likes acting human until he is sent to school.)

Balian, Lorna. *Leprechauns Never Lie*. Abingdon, 1980.

(In hopes of getting his pot of gold, Ninny Nanny captures a wee fairy man.)

Benton, Robert. *Don't Ever Wish for a 7-Foot Bear*. Illus. by Sally Benton. Knopf, 1972.

(A polar bear appears on Harold's doorstep, ready to cause trouble.)

Berger, Terry. *The Turtle's Picnic and Other Nonsense Stories*. Illus. by Erkki Alanen. Crown, 1977.

(Three stories introducing an untrusting baby turtle, a picky dog, and a boastful lion.)

Beskow, Elsa. *Pelle's New Suit*. Harper, 1929.

(Swedish story about making clothes from wool.)

Bishop, Claire. *The Five Chinese Brothers*. Illus. by Kurt Wiese. Coward, 1938.

(They can't be executed. Good to act out with improvised dialogue. However, the illustrations have been the source of a controversy about racial stereotyping, so consider carefully before reading.)

Blume, Judy. *The One in the Middle Is a Green Kangaroo*. Illus. by Amy Aitkin. Bradbury, 1981.

(Middle child makes his mark in the school play.)

Bollinger, Max. *The Most Beautiful Song*. Illus. by Jindra Capek. Little, 1981.

(King looks for a special singing bird.)

Bond, Michael. *Paddington Bear*. Illus. by Fred Banbery. Random, 1972.

(Easy introduction to irrepressible British bear. Look for other "Paddington" picture books in series.)

Brady, Irene. *Doodlebug*. Houghton, 1977.

(Jennifer's seemingly worthless new pony turns out to be quite valuable.)

Brenner, Barbara. *A Dog I Know*. Illus. by Fred Brenner. Harper, 1983.

(Quiet, insightful description, as told by the boy owner, of the qualities that make his dog unique. Children can write or tell about their own pets.)

————. *The Flying Patchwork Quilt*. Illus. by Fred Brenner. Scott, 1965.

(Little girl flies off wearing it, much to her brother's chagrin.)

Brown, Jeff. *Flat Stanley*. Illus. by Tomi Ungerer. Harper, 1964.
(Bulletin board flattens him. Use as a "What if...?" kick-off for creative writing. Read in two sittings.)

Brown, Marc. *Arthur's April Fool*. Little, 1983.
(Aardvark practices his new magic tricks while worrying about the school bully who's threatened to pulverize him.)
——————. *Arthur's Halloween*. Little, 1982.
(Halloween scares him until his little sister gives him courage.)

Brown, Margaret Wise. *Wheel on the Chimney*. Lippincott, 1954.
(Stork migration from Africa to Hungary. A Caldecott winner.)

Burnett, Carol. *What I Want To Be When I Grow Up*. Photos by Sheldon Secunda. Simon & Schuster, 1975.
(Carol Burnett in costume. Great writing incentive for career discussion.)

Burton, Virginia Lee. *The Little House*. Houghton, 1942.
(Growth of a town and the house that survives progress. A Caldecott winner and a natural for a social studies lesson on communities.)

Cameron, John. *If Mice Could Fly*. Atheneum, 1979.
(Mice best cats. In rhyme with wild illustrations.)

Cameron, Polly. *"I Can't," Said the Ant*. Coward, 1961.
(Crazy rhyming story and a natural poem starter.)

Carlson, Natalie Savage. *Marie Louise's Heyday*. Illus. by Jose Aruego and Ariane Dewey. Scribner, 1975.
(Mongoose babysits for five rambunctious opossums.)
——————. *The Night the Scarecrow Walked*. Illus. by Charles Robinson. Scribner, 1979.
(Spooky Halloween fare of two frightened children.)

Carroll, Ruth. *Tough Enough*. Oxford, 1954.
(Mischievous dog of Great Smoky Mountains family proves its worth.)

Caudill, Rebecca. *Did You Carry the Flag Today, Charlie?* Illus. by Nancy Grossman. Holt, 1966.
(Kentucky boy adjusts to kindergarten. Read in several installments.)

Chapman, Carol. *Barney Bipple's Magic Dandelions*. Illus. by Steven Kellogg. Dutton, 1977.
(Barney's wishes all come true, thanks to the lady next

door. Students can draw and tell what they would wish for.)

Charlip, Remy. *Fortunately,* Parents, 1964.
(After a series of misadventures, Jack makes it to his own surprise birthday party. Using the fortunate/unfortunate sequence of the story, children can retell it or make up their own individual or whole-class tales.)

Chess, Victoria. *Alfred's Alphabet Walk.* Greenwillow, 1979.
(Alliterative story starter that inspires imitation.)

Clifton, Lucille. *The Boy Who Didn't Believe in Spring.* Illus. by Brinton Turkle. Dutton, 1973.
(Inner-city boy and best friend search the neighborhood for proof.)

Cohen, Miriam. *Jim Meets the Thing.* Illus. by Lillian Hoban. Greenwillow, 1981.
(First grader faces his fears. Good discussion starter.)

Conford, Ellen. *Impossible, Possum.* Illus. by Rosemary Wells. Little, 1971.
(Opossum child is afraid to hang upside-down by his tail.)

Coombs, Patricia. *Dorrie and the Weather-Box.* Lothrop, 1966.
(Witch child causes a storm in the house. Look for other "Dorrie" books in series.)

Cooney, Barbara. *Miss Rumphius.* Viking, 1982.
(About the Lupine Lady from Maine who did something to make the world more beautiful. Spark a discussion of what we might do to improve the world. Wonderful for all ages.)

 Dahl, Roald. *The Enormous Crocodile.* Illus. by Quentin Blake. Knopf, 1978.
(Evil crocodile skulks about, looking for juicy children to eat.)

Dalgliesh, Alice. *The Bears on Hemlock Mountain.* Illus. by Helen Sewell. Scribner, 1952.
(Jonathan meets several on his way home from an errand for his mother.)

Desbarats, Peter. *Gabrielle and Selena.* Illus. by Nancy Grossman. Harcourt, 1968.
(Best friends switch houses and identities for a day.)

Devlin, Harry and Wende. *Cranberry Thanksgiving.* Parents, 1971.
(Includes Grandma's famous cranberry bread recipe.)
—————. *Old Black Witch.* Parents, 1972.
(Witch helps Nicky and his mother open the Jug and Muffin Tea Room.)

—————. *Old Witch Rescues Halloween.* Parents, 1972. (More Halloween fun as she teaches the town mayor a lesson.)

Dillon, Barbara. *The Teddy Bear Tree.* Illus. by David Rose. Morrow, 1982.
(After Bertine buries the eye from her missing teddy bear, a strange tree grows, bearing even stranger "fruit." Read in several sittings.)

Dragonwagon, Crescent. *I Hate My Brother Harry.* Illus. by Dick Gackenbach. Harper, 1983.
(Convinced that her older brother hates her, a little girl lists her reasons and thinks of a way to test his true feelings. Listeners will identify with this amusing look at a typical sibling relationship.)

Dyke, John. *Pigwig and the Pirates.* Methuen, 1979.
(Pig rescues nephew kidnapped by Captain Gruesome and crew.)

Elkin, Benjamin. *The Loudest Noise in the World.* Illus. by James Daugherty. Viking, 1954.
(Young prince of Hub-Bub wants to hear it. Follow up with a listening walk.)

Erickson, Russell E. *A Toad for Tuesday.* Illus. by Lawrence Di Fiori. Lothrop, 1974.
(Owl captures Warton for a birthday dinner. Look for others in series including *Warton and Morton*, 1976, *Warton and the Castaways*, 1982, *Warton and the King of the Skies*, 1978, and *Warton and the Traders*, 1979. Two or three sittings per book should do it.)

Fenton, Edward. *The Big Yellow Balloon.* Illus. by Ib Ohlsson. Doubleday, 1967.
(Chain reaction that occurs when cat chases Roger's giant balloon. Marvelous choice for creative drama with limited dialogue.)

Flack, Marjorie. *Walter the Lazy Mouse.* Illus. by Cyndy Szekeres. Doubleday, 1963.
(Rodent must fend for himself after his family moves away and forgets him. Read in chapter installments.)

Flora, James. *Leopold the See-Through Crumbpicker.* Harcourt, 1961.
(He's invisible and incorrigibly hungry. Have children draw how they think he looks before you reveal his picture.)

Freeman, Don. *Norman the Doorman.* Viking, 1959.
(Art museum mouse creates new sculpture. Students can make their own masterpieces.)

Garrett, Helen. *Angelo, the Naughty One.* Illus. by Leo Politi. Viking, 1944.
(On his sister's wedding day, a Mexican boy who hates baths runs away to avoid one.)

Giff, Patricia Reilly. *Today Was a Terrible Day.* Illus. by Susanna Natti. Viking, 1980.
(Everything goes wrong in school for a second grade boy.)

Hann, Jacquie. *That Man Is Talking to His Toes.* Four Winds, 1976.
(A whisper-down-the-lane story. Afterward, students can pass their own message down the row and see how it changes by the end.)

Harris, Dorothy Joan. *The School Mouse.* Illus. by Chris Conover. Warne, 1977.
(Boy brings verbal jeep-riding mouse to school.)

Heide, Florence Parry and Roxanne. *A Monster Is Coming! A Monster Is Coming!* Illus. by Rachi Farrow. Watts, 1980.
(Sister responds, "Don't bother me. I'm watching TV." Have children draw the monster as you read or show the illustrations and have them join in on the refrain. Also fun to act out in pairs.)

Hill, Elizabeth Starr. *Evan's Corner.* Illus. by Nancy Grossman. Holt, 1967.
(In the family's small apartment, Evan needs a space to call his own.)

Hiller, Catherine. *Abracatabby.* Illus. by Victoria de Larrea. Coward, 1981.
(Magical cat shows off at a birthday party.)

Hoban, Tana. *Look Again!* Macmillan, 1971.
(Partially hidden photos to identify. Children can create their own.)

Hurwitz, Johanna. *Busybody Nora.* Illus. by Susan Jeschke. Morrow, 1976.
(Anecdotes about a young girl and her family in their N.Y.C. apartment. Also try *New Neighbors for Nora*, 1979, Read a chapter or two a day.)

————. *Superduper Teddy.* Illus. by Susan Jeschke. Morrow, 1980.
(Nora's shy little brother matures in kindergarten. Short chapters.)

Hutchins, Pat. *One-Eyed Jake.* Greenwillow, 1979.
(Mean pirate gets what he deserves.)

————. *The Tale of Thomas Mead.* Greenwillow, 1980.
(Boy refuses to read. "Why should I?" he declares. In

rhyme.)

Jeffers, Susan. *Wild Robin*. Dutton, 1976.
(Bad boy is captured by Fairy Queen. Based on Scottish Ballad, "Tamlane.")

Johnson, Crockett. *Harold's Trip to the Sky*. Harper, 1957.
(The purple crayon kid strikes again. Draw your own new adventures.)

Johnston, Johanna. *Speak Up, Edie*. Illus. by Paul Galdone. Putnam, 1974.
(Chatterbox gets a big part in the Thanksgiving play.)

Jonas, Ann. *Round Trip*. Greenwillow, 1983.
(A journey from home into the city and back again. Striking black and white graphics are all the more remarkable when, halfway through the journey, you turn the book upside down for the return trip. Children may want to design their own two-way drawings. Fascinating for all ages.)

Joslin, Sesyle. *What Do You Do, Dear?* Illus. by Maurice Sendak. Scott, 1961.
(Wacky approach to manners. Students can think up new situations. Fun for acting out in pairs.)

————. *What Do You Say, Dear?* Illus. by Maurice Sendak. Scott, 1958.
(More awkward encounters involving manners. Also fine to act out in pairs.)

Keats, Ezra Jack. *Regards to the Man in the Moon*. Four Winds, 1981.
(Children travel through space via their imaginations.)

Kellogg, Steven. *The Mysterious Tadpole*. Dial, 1977.
(Boy's new pet gets huge. The Weston Woods filmstrip version is delightful.)

————. *Pinkerton, Behave*. Dial, 1979.
(Ungainly Great Dane flunks obedience school, but gets the burglar anyway.)

Kennedy, Richard. *The Contests at Cowlick*. Illus. by Marc Simont. Little, 1975.
(Plucky boy outwits the outlaws who want to tear up the town.)

Kessler, Leonard. *Old Turtle's Baseball Stories*. Greenwillow, 1982.
(Funny animal tales of bat and ball.)

Krauss, Ruth. *Is This You?* Illus. by Crockett Johnson. Scholastic, 1968 (pbk. only).
(How to make a book about yourself. A good starter for young authors.)

Kroll, Steven. *Amanda and the Giggling Ghost.* Illus. by Dick Gackenbach. Holiday, 1980.
(Little girl is blamed for a ghost's thefts.)

————. *Friday the 13th.* Illus. by Dick Gackenbach. Holiday, 1981.
(About the misfortunes of Harold, whose luck finally changes for the better.)

————. *The Tyrannosaurus Game.* Illus. by Tomie de Paola. Holiday, 1976.
(A group of children spin a yarn. Your students can conjure up their own.)

Lauber, Patricia. *Clarence and the Burglar.* Illus. by Paul Galdone. Coward, 1973.
(Beagle becomes a hero when he unwittingly thwarts a robbery.)

Lewis, Eils Moorhouse. *The Snug Little House.* Illus. by Elise Primavera. Atheneum, 1981.
(Chair, table, bed, dishes, and silverware go down the road a piece and settle in a house. Good for narrative pantomime or improvised dialogue.)

Lewis, Thomas P. *Hill of Fire.* Illus. by Joan Sandin. Harper, 1971.
(How an ordinary Mexican farmer discovered a volcano growing in his cornfield. A fictionalized version of the birth of Paricutin in 1943.)

Lexau, Joan. *Benjie.* Illus. by Don Bolognese. Dial, 1964.
(Shy boy finds his grandmother's lost earring and gains confidence in the process.)

————. *I'll Tell on You.* Illus. by Gail Owens. Dutton, 1976.
(After his dog bites a little girl, Mark is afraid to admit it. Good discussion starter.)

Lifton, Betty Jean. *Good Night, Orange Monster.* Illus. by Cyndy Szekeres. Atheneum, 1972.
(Boy is afraid of monsters in the closet until he makes friends with one.)

Lindgren, Astrid. *The Tomten.* Illus. by Harald Wiberg. Coward, 1962.
(Winter story about the nocturnal elf-like little creature in the barn.)

Lindgren, Barbro. *The Wild Baby.* Illus. by Eva Eriksson. Greenwillow, 1981.
(Mischief-making baby boy causes his loving mother her share of grief. In rhyme.)

Lionni, Leo. *Alexander and the Wind-Up Mouse*. Pantheon, 1969.
(Mouse looks for the magic pebble that will turn his toy mouse friend real.)

————. *Frederick*. Pantheon, 1967.
(Mouse poet's imagery sustains his friends through a long harsh winter.)

Lobel, Arnold. *Owl at Home*. Harper, 1975.
(Five short episodes of winter, bumps in the night, tear-water tea, being in two places at the same time, and a moon friend. Listeners can add sad ideas for making more tea.)

————. *A Treeful of Pigs*. Illus. by Anita Lobel. Greenwillow, 1979.
(A lazy farmer is tricked by his clever wife into doing his chores.)

————. *Uncle Elephant*. Harper, 1981.
(When a young elephant's parents are lost at sea, he is taken in by his uncle.)

Long, Claudia. *Albert's Story*. Illus. by Judy Glasser. Delacorte, 1978.
(Boy expands his one-sentence story. Students can make up their own.)

Lord, John Vernon. *The Giant Jam Sandwich*. Houghton, 1973.
(Poem-story about a wasp-filled town.)

Low, Alice. *The Witch Who Was Afraid of Witches*. Illus. by Karen Gundersheimer. Pantheon, 1978.
(The youngest witch in the family finds her own special powers.)

Low, Joseph. *Mice Twice*. Atheneum, 1980.
(Cat and mouse plot and counterplot to eat and avoid being eaten.)

Lystad, Mary. *Jennifer Takes Over P.S. 94*. Illus. by Ray Cruz. Putnam, 1972.
(Girl imagines how she'd run her school. Your students will have plenty of ideas, too.)

Mahy, Margaret. *The Boy Who Was Followed Home*. Illus. by Steven Kellogg. Watts, 1975.
(Robert needs a witch's help to rid him of the 27 hippos on his lawn.)

Marshall, Edward. *Space Case*. Illus. by James Marshall. Dial, 1980.
(This critter visited Earth before E.T. Read for Halloween and have children invent their own space creatures.)

—————. *Troll Country*. Illus. by James Marshall. Dial, 1980.
(Elsie Fay tricks a troll.)

Matsuno, Masako. *A Pair of Red Clogs*. Illus. by Kazue Mizamura. World, 1960.
(Japanese girl breaks her beautiful new clogs and is afraid to admit it to her mother.)

Mayer, Mercer. *Liza Lou and the Yeller Belly Swamp*. Parents, 1976.
(Spunky girl outsmarts the creatures she meets while doing errands for Mama.)

—————. *Mrs. Beggs and the Wizard*. Four Winds, 1973.
(Wizard wreaks havoc in Mrs. Beggs's boarding house.)

McCloskey, Robert. *Make Way for Ducklings*. Viking, 1941.
(Mallard parents look for a suitable Boston site in which to raise their family. A Caldecott winner.)

McNaughton, Colin. *Anton B. Stanton and the Pirats*. Benn, 1979.
(Swashbuckling miniature boy fights evil pirate rodents.)

—————. *The Rat Race*. Doubleday, 1978.
(Miniature boy, Anton, is jailed in a rat kingdom.)

McPhail, David. *Great Cat*. Dutton, 1982.
(Toby and the biggest cat ever rescue stranded children from the ocean.)

Modell, Frank. *Tooley! Tooley!* Greenwillow, 1979.
(Two boys look for a lost dog and find mutts galore in their search.)

Myller, Rolf. *A Very Noisy Day*. Atheneum, 1981.
(A typical day in one dog's life, full of noises children will love to make as you read.)

Ness, Evaline. *Sam, Bangs and Moonshine*. Holt, 1966.
(Little girl tells one wild story too many. A Caldecott winner.)

Nikly, Michelle. *The Emperor's Plum Tree*. Greenwillow, 1982.
(Seeking perfection, the emperor looks for another plum tree to be planted in his garden.)

Nixon, Joan Lowery. *Gloria Chipmunk, Star!* Illus. by Diane Dawson. Houghton, 1980.
(Chipmunk finds a way to take care of her baby brother and still be in the class play.)

Noble, Trinka Hakes. *The Day Jimmy's Boa Ate the Wash*. Illus. by Steven Kellogg. Dial, 1980.
(Wild class trip to a farm sets off a chain of silly disasters.)

Nolan, Dennis. *Witch Bazooza*. Prentice, 1979.

(Witch uses gourds to decorate her house for Halloween.)

Parkin, Rex. *The Red Carpet*. Macmillan, 1948.

(Hotel carpet unrolls all through the town. Related in rollicking rhyme.)

Peet, Bill. *Big Bad Bruce*. Houghton, 1977.

(Bear bully is tamed by Roxy, a no-nonsense witch.)

——————. *Cyrus the Unsinkable Sea Serpent*. Houghton, 1975.

(Peaceful sea monster protects sailing ship from ocean disasters.)

——————. *Encore for Eleanor*. Houghton, 1981.

(Retired circus elephant learns to draw.)

——————. *Hubert's Hair-Raising Adventure*. Houghton, 1959.

(Rhyming saga of the overwhelming replacement of a lion's burned locks.

——————. *The Spooky Tail of Prewett Peacock*. Houghton, 1972.

(Outcast peacock redeems himself when his strange feather formation saves the day.)

Peppe, Rodney. *The Mice Who Lived in a Shoe*. Lothrop, 1981.

(Mice build a new house using a human shoe as their frame. Children can design their own mouse dream houses.)

Peterson, Esther Allen. *Frederick's Alligator*. Illus. by Susanna Natti. Crown, 1979.

(Boy finds a baby one, though no one will believe him.)

——————. *Penelope Gets Wheels*. Illus. by Susanna Natti. Crown, 1982.

(Girl finds her new roller skates are the best wheels a kid can have.)

Prelutsky, Jack. *The Terrible Tiger*. Illus. by Arnold Lobel. Macmillan, 1970.

(He sings his terrible song in verse and swallows a baker, a grocer, and worse. While similar to Jack Kent's *The Fat Cat* and other folktales of greedy swallowing creatures, this story boasts a wicked chorus for children to chant or sing.)

Rayner, Mary. *Garth Pig and the Ice Cream Lady*. Atheneum, 1977.

(Mrs. Wolf abducts Garth while his nine piglet siblings rush to the rescue.)

——————. *Mr. and Mrs. Pig's Evening Out*. Atheneum, 1976.

(Wicked Mrs. Wolf is the ten piglets' new babysitter.)
—————. *Mrs. Pig's Bulk Buy*. Atheneum, 1981.
(Piglets are cured of their ketchup overdoses when their mother feeds them nothing but.)

Rose, Anne. *The Triumphs of Fuzzy Fogtop*. Illus. by Tomie de Paola. Dial, 1979.
(Three stories of a foolish man, loosely based on Jewish folktales.)

Ross, Pat. *M and M and the Haunted House Game*. Illus. by Marilyn Hafner. Pantheon, 1980.
(Two girls scare each other silly. Follow up by making a sound tape of scary noises with your students.)

Ryan, Cheli Duran. *Hildilid's Night*. Illus. by Arnold Lobel. Macmillan, 1971.
(Old woman tries to chase away the night.)

Say, Allen. *The Bicycle Man*. Houghton, 1982.
(A reminiscence from the author's childhood in postwar Japan, of the time two American soldiers entertained the entire school at the end of the sportsday festivities.)

Schwartz, Amy. *Bea and Mr. Jones*. Bradbury, 1982.
(Kindergarten girl and dad switch jobs. Good writing lead-into "What if *you* switched jobs with your mom or dad?")

Schweitzer, Byrd Baylor. *Amigo*. Illus. by Garth Williams. Macmillan, 1963.
(Narrative poem of desert boy and prairie dog who tame each other.)

Segal, Lore. *Tell Me a Mitzi*. Illus. by Harriet Pincus. Farrar, 1970.
(Three family stories of visiting Grandma, catching colds, and calling back a parade.)
—————. *Tell Me a Trudy*. Illus. by Rosemary Wells. Farrar, 1977.
(Three more family stories of copycatting, sharing, and robbers in the bathroom.)

Selden, George. *Sparrow Socks*. Illus. by Peter Lippman. Harper, 1965.
(Scottish sock factory caters to the birds. Read with your best brogue.)

Seuling, Barbara. *The Triplets*. Houghton, 1980.
(Three indistinguishable sisters want to be recognized as individuals.)

Seuss, Dr. *Horton Hatches the Egg*. Random, 1940.
(Accommodating elephant helps a lazy bird. In verse.)
—————. *Horton Hears a Who!* Random, 1954.

(Elephant discovers tiny dust-planet in need of protection. In verse.)

——————. *How the Grinch Stole Christmas*. Random, 1957.

(Evil Grinch steals all the presents in Who-ville. In rhyme.)

——————. *If I Ran the Zoo*. Random, 1950.

(Lots of looney animals. Your students can make up more of the same.)

——————. *The King's Stilts*. Random, 1939.

(Eric, a page boy, returns the king's beloved stilts in time to save the kingdom from the terrible Nizzards.)

Illustration from MY UNCLE PODGER by Wallace Tripp. Original text and illustrations copyright © 1975 by Wallace Tripp. Reproduced by permission of Little, Brown and Company.

————. *McElligot's Pool.* Random, 1947.
(Boy imagines all the wild fish he could catch. Children will love making up their own unique species.)

————. *On Beyond Zebra.* Random, 1955.
(Crazy new alphabet letters. Invent your own new alphabets.)

Sharmat, Marjorie Weinman. *The Best Valentine in the World.* Illus. by Lilian Obligado. Holiday, 1982.
(Ferdinand Fox makes one for his friend, Florette. Read the first week in February and then design your own gorgeous valentines.)

————. *Gila Monsters Meet You at the Airport.* Illus. by Byron Barton. Macmillan, 1980.
(Boy moves out West, expecting the worst. Good discussion starter on preconceived notions.)

————. *Gladys Told Me To Meet Her Here.* Illus. by Edward Frascino. Harper, 1970.
(Irving looks for his best friend and imagines where she might be.)

————. *Nate the Great.* Illus. by Marc Simont. Coward, 1972.
(Amateur boy detective solves his first mystery. Use as an introduction to the rest of this delightful hard-boiled series.)

Sharmat, Mitchell. *Gregory the Terrible Eater.* Illus. by Jose Aruego and Ariane Dewey. Four Winds, 1980.
(Goat parents worry when their son won't eat junk. Your class can make up a new week's menu for either Gregory or themselves.)

Shub, Elizabeth. *Seeing Is Believing.* Illus. by Rachel Isadora. Greenwillow, 1979.
(Farm boy meets up with a tricky leprechaun and horse-riding pixies. A natural for St. Patrick's Day.)

Silverstein, Shel. *A Giraffe and a Half.* Harper, 1964.
(In the style of "The House That Jack Built" involving a boy's giraffe and many ridiculous add-on rhymes. Ideal for recalling sequence and inspiring snickers.)

————. *Who Wants a Cheap Rhinoceros?* Macmillan, 1983.
(What to do with one when you get it. Have your students come up with new uses.)

Skurzynski, Gloria. *Martin by Himself.* Illus. by Lynn Munsinger. Houghton, 1979.
(Boy makes a mess at home on the day his mother goes back to work.)

Smith, Janice Lee. *The Monster in the Third Dresser Drawer and Other Stories About Adam Joshua.* Illus. by Dick Gackenbach. Harper, 1981.
(A young boy copes with moving, a new sister, a new tooth, and other daily mishaps. Short chapters.)

Spier, Peter. *Bored, Nothing To Do.* Doubleday, 1978.
(Two brothers scour the house for parts to the airplane they are building.)

Spinelli, Eileen. *Thanksgiving at the Tappletons'.* Illus. by Maryann Cocca-Leffler. Addison, 1982.
(Just because there are no turkey and trimmings doesn't mean the family gives up on their holiday dinner.)

Stadler, John. *Animal Cafe.* Bradbury, 1980.
(When the human owner leaves at night, the animals take over the restaurant.)

Steig, William. *Sylvester and the Magic Pebble.* Simon & Schuster, 1959.
(Donkey regrets it when his wish comes true. A Caldecott winner.)

Stevenson, James. *Could Be Worse.* Greenwillow, 1977.
(Grandpa spins a wild yarn. Great to act out as a group pantomime.)

————. *That Terrible Halloween Night.* Greenwillow, 1980.
(Grandpa describes the fright of his life. Have your students draw and describe what they think Grandpa found behind that door.)

————. *We Can't Sleep.* Greenwillow, 1982.
(Another exciting Grandpa story to read and act out in pantomime.)

————. *What's Under My Bed?* Greenwillow, 1983.
(When Mary Ann and Louie are afraid of night noises and can't sleep, Grandpa recalls a similar experience from his own childhood.)

Taylor, Mark. *The Case of the Missing Kittens.* Illus. by Graham Booth. Atheneum, 1978.
(Angus the dog solves the mystery.)

Titus, Eve. *Anatole.* Illus. by Paul Galdone. McGraw, 1956.
(French mouse creates his own job as a taster at a local cheese factory.)

Tobias, Tobi. *Chasing the Goblins Away.* Illus. by Victor Ambrus. Warne, 1977.
(Boy is terrified of night goblins until he fights them back.)

Torgersen, Don Arthur. *The Girl Who Tricked the Troll.* Illus.

by Tom Dunnington. Childrens, 1978.
(Karin must think of a question that he can't answer.)

Tresselt, Alvin. *Hide and Seek Fog.* Illus. by Roger DuVoisin. Lothrop, 1965.
(Fog at the seashore.)

Viorst, Judith. *My Mama Says There Aren't Any Zombies, Ghosts, Vampires, Creatures, Demons, Monsters, Fiends, Goblins or Things.* Illus. by Kay Chorao. Atheneum, 1973.
(But mamas aren't always right. Have listeners chime in on the spooky sound effects.)

Waber, Bernard. *An Anteater Named Arthur.* Houghton, 1967.
(What he is really like, as told by his mother. Children can discuss how they think their mothers would describe them.)

——————. *Lovable Lyle.* Houghton, 1969.
(Lyle the Crocodile has an unknown enemy. One of a series.)

——————. *Lyle Finds His Mother.* Houghton, 1974.
(New York City crocodile meets up with his former manager who convinces him to search for his long–lost parent.)

Wagner, Jenny. *John Brown, Rose and the Midnight Cat.* Illus. by Ron Brooks. Bradbury, 1977.
(Old woman's jealous sheepdog tries to thwart the stray cat from staying.)

Ward, Lynd. *The Biggest Bear.* Houghton, 1952.
(Johnny brings home a baby bear who grows. A Caldecott winner.)

Waterton, Betty. *Petranella.* Illus. by Ann Blades. Vanguard, 1980.
(On her way to the new family homestead in Canada, girl loses the flower seeds her grandmother gave her.)

——————. *A Salmon for Simon.* Illus. by Ann Blades. Atheneum, 1980.
(Canadian boy saves a salmon dropped by an eagle.)

Watson, Clyde. *How Brown Mouse Kept Christmas.* Illus. by Wendy Watson. Farrar, 1980.
(Attic mouse explores downstairs on Christmas Eve.)

Williams, Vera. *A Chair for My Mother.* Greenwillow, 1982.
(After the fire that has destroyed all their belongings, a girl, her mother, and grandmother save change in a jar until they can buy a new chair. Vibrant illustrations.)

——————. *Something Special for Me.* Greenwillow, 1983.

(Rosa shops for her own perfect birthday present. Charming sequel to *A Chair for My Mother.)*

Withers, Carl. *Tale of a Black Cat.* Holt, 1966.

(A draw-as-you-tell story. Hand out paper and black crayons so that your students can follow as you draw the story on the blackboard.)

————. *The Wild Ducks and the Goose.* Holt, 1968.

(A draw-as-you-tell story of a foolish man.)

Zelinsky, Paul. *The Maid and the Mouse and the Odd-Shaped House.* Dodd, 1981.

(Another drawing story in rhyme and a variant of Withers's *Tale of a Black Cat.* Use both and compare.)

Illustration "Grandpa in the grip of a giant lobster" from COULD BE WORSE! by James Stevenson. Copyright © 1977 by James Stevenson. Reproduced by permission of Greenwillow Books (A Division of William Morrow & Company).

Read-Aloud Fiction
for Grades 2–3

Anderson, Lonzo. *The Ponies of Mykillengi*. Illus. by Adrienne Adams. Scribner, 1966.
(Icelandic children and ponies brave a winter storm.)

Annett, Cora. *How the Witch Got Alf*. Illus. by Steven Kellogg. Watts, 1975.
(Donkey craves affection and runs away when he doesn't get enough.)

Barrett, Judi. *Animals Should Definitely Not Wear Clothing*. Illus. by Ron Barrett. Atheneum, 1970.
(Lots of reasons why. Hilarious writing incentive.)

——————. *Cloudy with a Chance of Meatballs*. Illus. by Ron Barrett. Atheneum, 1978.
(Town undergoes a crisis when normal edible weather turns nasty. Read after a weather lesson for a bizarre literary twist.)

Bennet, Anna Elizabeth. *Little Witch*. Illus. by Helen Stone. Lippincott, 1953.
(Witch's child rebels and sneaks off to school with normal children. Chapters.)

Blume, Judy. *Freckle Juice*. Illus. by Sonia O. Lisker. Four Winds, 1971.
(Andrew will try anything to get freckles. Read in two installments.)

Brooks, Walter Rollin. *Jimmy Takes Vanishing Lessons*. Illus. by Don Bolognese. Knopf, 1965.
(Jimmy befriends a timid ghost who haunts a deserted house. Two sittings.)

Brown, Margaret Wise. *The Important Book*. Illus. by Leonard Weisgard. Harper, 1949.
(Descriptions of why various objects are important. Good writing starter.)

Bulla, Clyde Robert. *The Sword in the Tree*. Illus. by Paul Galdone. Crowell, 1956.
(In the days of King Arthur, a young boy's uncle proves himself a wicked knight. Chapters.)

Calhoun, Mary. *Cross-Country Cat*. Illus. by Erick Ingraham. Morrow, 1979.
(Siamese feline on skis makes it down the mountain.)

——————. *The Goblin Under the Stairs*. Illus. by Janet McCaffery. Morrow, 1968.
(A hairy boggart causes mayhem in a Yorkshire farm-

house until the farmwife treats him right.)

—————. *The Night the Monster Came.* Illus. by Leslie Morrill. Morrow, 1982.

(Boy fears Bigfoot has left the footprints outside the house. Chapters.)

Cameron, Ann. *The Stories Julian Tells.* Illus. by Ann Strugnell. Pantheon, 1981.

(Wonderful family anecdotes of two brothers and their parents. Chapters.)

Catling, Patrict Skene. *The Chocolate Touch.* Illus. by Margot Apple. Morrow, 1979.

(Modern-day Midas story of a greedy boy who can't resist candy. Chapters.)

Charlip, Remy. *Harlequin and the Gift of Many Colors.* Parents, 1973.

(Lyrical story of the first harlequin.)

Cleary, Beverly. *Beezus and Ramona.* Illus. by Louis Darling. Morrow, 1955.

(Beezus must learn to cope with the world's brattiest little sister. Chapters.)

—————. *Henry Huggins.* Illus. by Louis Darling. Morrow, 1950.

(When Henry finds a mutt, getting him home is just the first problem. Chapters.)

—————. *Ramona the Pest.* Illus. by Louis Darling. Morrow, 1968.

(Kindergarten is Ramona's newest challenge. Chapters.)

—————. *Ribsy.* Illus. by Louis Darling. Morrow, 1964.

(Henry Huggins's dog gets lost. Chapters.)

Cohen, Barbara. *The Carp in the Bathtub.* Illus. by Joan Halpern. Lothrop, 1972.

(Children try to save live Passover fish from becoming gefilte fish.)

Cole, Brock. *The King at the Door.* Doubleday, 1979.

(Little Baggit believes the begger at the inn is the king.)

—————. *Nothing but a Pig.* Doubleday, 1981.

(Pig aspires to a more dignified life.)

Coletta, Irene. *From A to Z: The Collected Letters of Irene and Hallie Coletta.* Prentice, 1979.

(Marvelous alphabet rebus poems. Have your children compose and illustrate their own.)

Coombs, Patricia. *Molly Mullett.* Lothrop, 1975.

(Unflappable girl defeats a ferocious ogre.)

Corbett, Scott. *Steady, Freddie!* Illus. by Lawrence Beall Smith. Dutton, 1970.

(Donna loses her pet frog in an empty box at the Girl Scout cookie factory. Chapters.)

Coren, Alan. *Arthur the Kid*. Illus. by John Astrop. Little, 1977.
(Boy shapes up a gang of incompetent outlaws. One of a tongue-in-cheek series, including *Buffalo Arthur*, 1978, *The Lone Arthur*, 1977, and *Railroad Arthur*, 1978.)

Dahl, Roald. *The Fantastic Mr. Fox*. Illus. by Donald Chaffin. Knopf, 1970.
(How a fox outfoxes three vengeful hunters. Chapters.)

————. *The Magic Finger*. Illus. by William Pène du Bois. Harper, 1966.
(Antihunting tale of a girl with a diabolical digit. Read in two sittings.)

Daugherty, James. *Andy and the Lion*. Viking, 1938.
(A modern companion to the Greek tale of Androcles, who dethorns a lion's paw. Try acting out Part Two in pairs pantomime.)

De Paola, Tomie. *Big Anthony and the Magic Ring*. Harcourt, 1979.
(Strega Nona's bumbling assistant finds a way to become handsome.)

————. *Strega Nona's Magic Lessons*. Harcourt, 1982.
(Big Anthony disguises himself as a girl so that Strega Nona will instruct him, too.)

Dillon, Barbara. *What's Happened to Harry?* Illus. by Chris Conover. Morrow, 1982.
(Witch Hepzibah the Hateful turns him into a poodle on Halloween night. Chapters.)

Du Bois, William Pene. *Lazy Tommy Pumpkinhead*. Harper, 1966.
(Machines run his life until the power fails. Act out the machinery as a group.)

Embry, Margaret. *The Blue-Nosed Witch*. Illus. by Carl Rose. Holiday, 1956.
(Witch child with lighted proboscis goes trick-or-treating with human children. Chapters.)

Feagles, Anita. *Casey, the Utterly Impossible Horse*. Illus. by Dagmar Wilson. Scholastic, 1960 (pbk. only).
(Talking horse wants his own striped pajamas for a start. Chapters.)

Fleischman, Sid. *The Ghost on Saturday Night*. Illus. by Eric von Schmidt. Little, 1974.
(Scoundrel who claims to be able to raise the ghost of Crookneck John has a shady motive.)

Illustration from ANDY AND THE LION by James Daugherty. Copyright 1938, renewed copyright © 1966 by James Daugherty. Reproduced by permission of Viking Penguin, Inc.

Flora, James. *Grandpa's Ghost Stories*. Atheneum, 1978.
(Funny spine ticklers. Students can write their own Grandpa adventures.)
──────────. *Grandpa's Witched-Up Christmas*. Atheneum, 1982.
(Nasty witch turns boy into porker.)
──────────. *The Great Green Turkey Creek Monster*. Atheneum, 1976.
(Great Green Hooligan Vine escapes and overtakes the town. This wild story would make a great detailed mural for your walls.)
──────────. *The Joking Man*. Harcourt, 1968.
(Wild and crazy stunts are pulled when the mysterious Joking Man comes to town. Before you reveal the ending, have your students draw a quick sketch of their vision of this character.)
──────────. *Little Hatchy Hen*. Harcourt, 1969.
(Hen that can hatch outlandish items is kidnapped.)
──────────. *My Friend Charlie*. Harcourt, 1964.
(Two wacky boys. A good chapter for writing skills: "Things NOT to do.")
Gaeddert, Lou Ann. *Gustav the Gourmet Giant*. Illus. by Steven Kellogg. Dial, 1976.
(Gluttony kills him when he decides to eat boy for dinner.)
Gammell, Stephen. *Once Upon MacDonald's Farm*. Four Winds, 1981.
(He gets zoo animals for his farm. Try reading with a straight face, if you can.)
Gauch, Patricia Lee. *This Time, Tempe Wick?* Illus. by Margot Tomes. Coward, 1974.
(N.J. colonial heroine hid her horse in her bedroom to save it from looting soldiers.)
Gerstein, Mordicai. *Arnold of the Ducks*. Harper, 1983.
(Little boy raised by ducks almost becomes one until chance reunites him with his human family. Act out Arnold's duck training in pantomime with your class.)
Graeber, Charlotte. *Mustard*. Illus. by Donna Diamond. Macmillan, 1982.
(Alex's wonderful old cat sickens and dies. Sad, but beautifully handled. Read in two sittings.)
Green, Melinda. *Rachel's Recital*. Little, 1979.
(Girl who hates to practice neglects to learn her piano piece in time. Chapters.)
Hall, Donald. *Ox-cart Man*. Illus. by Barbara Cooney. Viking, 1979.

(Cycle of seasons on a nineteenth century farm. A Caldecott winner.)

Hall, Malcolm. *Headlines.* Illus. by Wallace Tripp. Coward, 1973.
(Animal newspaper. Have your students decode the baffling headlines in the story and then think up new ones.)

Hirsch, Marilyn. *Potato Pancakes All Around.* Bonim, 1978.
("Stone Soup" variant for Hanukkah. Get out your frying pan!)

Hoban, Tana. *Take Another Look.* Greenwillow, 1981.
(Your children can make their own photo surprises after guessing these.)

Hurwitz, Johanna. *Aldo Applesauce.* Illus. by John Wallner. Morrow, 1979.
(Boy moves to the suburbs and gains a new nickname. Chapters.)

——————. *Much Ado About Aldo.* Illus. by John Wallner. Morrow, 1978.
(Aldo becomes a vegetarian. Chapters.)

Johnson, Elizabeth. *Stuck with Luck.* Illus. by Trina Schart Hyman. Little, 1967.
(Magruder McGillicuddy O'Toole, a leprechaun on vacation in the U.S., can't go home again until he gets his lilt back.)

Julian, Nancy R. *The Peculiar Miss Pickett.* Illus. by Donald E. Cooke. Winston, 1951.
(American Mary Poppins with magic eyes. Read a chapter a day.)

Keats, Ezra Jack. *Apt. 3.* Macmillan, 1971.
(Sounds of an apartment house. Introspective and a good spur for discussion.)

Kellogg, Steven. *The Island of the Skog.* Dial, 1976.
(Mice searching for peace from cats sail to an island with its own monster.)

Kroll, Steven. *Space Cats.* Illus. by Friso Henstra. Holiday, 1979.
(Cat war on the planet Floralderon and the Earth boy who comes to help. Chapters.)

Levy, Elizabeth. *Frankenstein Moved in on the Fourth Floor.* Illus. by Mordicai Gerstein. Harper, 1979.
(Sam and Robert investigate their scary new neighbor. Chapters.)

Lionni, Leo. *Tico and the Golden Wings.* Pantheon, 1964.
(Wingless bird is granted his wish. Good discussion starter.)

Lobel, Arnold. *The Ice Cream Cone Coot and Other Rare Birds.* Parents, 1971.
(Humorous rhyming ditties about unique feathered flyers. Children love to create their own. Try switching animals, such as Marshmallowed Malamutes or Sandpaper Siamese.)

MacDonald, Betty. *Mrs. Piggle-Wiggle.* Illus. by Hilary Knight. Lippincott, 1947.
(She cures all those bad habits children have that drive adults crazy. Read a chapter a day, and perhaps your students will become angels, too.)

Massie, Diane Redfield. *Chameleon Was a Spy.* Crowell, 1979.
(Chameleon comes to the rescue when a pickle company's magic formula disappears.)

Matthews, Louise. *Gator Pie.* Illus. by Jeni Bassett. Dodd, 1979.
(Fractured fraction fun to introduce a day's math lesson.)

Mayer, Mercer. *A Special Trick.* Dial, 1970.
(Elroy tries out a magician's monster-filled book of magic spells.)

Illustration by Ib Ohlsson from THE BIG YELLOW BALLOON by Edward Fenton. Copyright © 1967 by Doubleday & Company, Inc. Reproduced by permission of the publisher.

McCarthy, Agnes. *Room 10*. Illus. by Ib Ohlsson. Doubleday, 1966.
(A year in the life of one third grade class. A natural end-of-the-year motivator for recording your own class adventures.)

McCloskey, Robert. *Burt Dow, Deep-Water Man*. Viking, 1963.
(Maine fisherman catches and is swallowed by a whale. In the whale's belly, Burt creates a Jackson Pollack-like painting. Try your hands at spatter paintings.)

—————. *Lentil*. Macmillan, 1940.
(Boy's harmonica saves the day. Bring in lemons for your students to suck.)

—————. *Time of Wonder*. Viking, 1957.
(Poetic description of the end of summer on a Maine island. Ask your students to describe their special places.)

Mendoza, George. *A Wart Snake in a Fig Tree*. Illus. by Etienne Delessert. Dial, 1968.
(Parody of "The Twelve Days of Christmas." Sing along and then have everyone come up with new versions.)

Milne, A.A. *The House at Pooh Corner*. Illus. by Ernest H. Shepard. Dutton, 1928.
(Everyone's favorite bear. Tiddly pom. Read a chapter a day.)

—————. *Winnie-the-Pooh*. Illus. by Ernest H. Shepard. Dutton, 1926.
(In which we meet Pooh Bear and the other animals in the Hundred Acre Wood. Read a chapter a day.)

Monjo, F.N. *The Drinking Gourd*. Illus. by Fred Brenner. Harper, 1970.
(Boy and father help slaves escape on the Underground Railroad.)

Moore, Lilian. *The Snake That Went to School*. Illus. by Mary Stevens. Random, 1957.
(Hank's pet hognose snake disappears when he takes it to school. Chapters.)

Myller, Rolf. *How Big Is a Foot?* Atheneum, 1969.
(Clever story of measurement. After reading it aloud, assign your children the task of measuring everything in sight. How long are their feet? How about the length of the whole school?)

Nixon, Joan Lowery. *If You Say So, Claude*. Illus. by Lorinda Bryan Cauley. Warne, 1980.
(Frontier Texas tall tale of a couple looking for the perfect spot to settle.)

Parish, Peggy. *Amelia Bedelia*. Illus. by Fritz Siebel. Harper, 1963.
(Looney maid takes everything literally. Look for other books in the series. Students can write their own episodes using literal language.)

Peet, Bill. *Capyboppy*. Houghton, 1966.
(True story of Peet's son's capybara, a giant rodent that makes a demanding pet.)

—————. *Cowardly Clyde*. Houghton, 1979.
(Knight's terrified horse proves his mettle when he tangles with an ogre.)

—————. *The Gnats of Knotty Pine*. Houghton, 1975.
(Gnats foil hunters from shooting their prey.)

—————. *No Such Things*. Houghton, 1983.
(Rhymes about outrageous creatures such as Glubzunks, Juggarums, and Grabnabbits. Similar in scope to Arnold Lobel's *The Ice-Cream Cone Coot*. Children can invent new animals and rhymes to go along.)

Pomerantz, Charlotte. *The Downtown Fairy Godmother*. Illus. by Susanna Natti. Addison, 1978.
(After wishing for a beautiful stuffed black cat, Olivia meets her own Grade C Fairy Godmother, pink curlers and all.)

Prelutsky, Jack. *The Mean Old Mean Hyena*. Illus. by Arnold Lobel. Greenwillow, 1978.
(Wickedly funny poem-story of a nasty hyena who does not learn his lesson.)

Rinkoff, Barbara. *The Dragon's Handbook*. Illus. by Kelly Oechsli. Nelson, 1966.
(Boy finds it and convinces the dragon to teach him a spell. Chapters.)

—————. *The Remarkable Ramsey*. Illus. by Leonard Shortall. Morrow, 1965.
(Boy meets talking dog who cures him of being shy. Also a 1976 Scholastic paperback, retitled *Remarkable Ramsey, the Talking Dog*. Chapters.)

Robinson, Nancy K. *Just Plain Cat*. Four Winds, 1983.
(Chris survives the traumas of third grade, from getting a screamer for a teacher to having trouble with his new cat. Chapters.)

Rosen, Winifred. *Ralph Proves the Pudding*. Illus. by Lionel Kalish. Doubleday, 1972.
(Boy makes a TV commercial. Makes a great truth-in-advertising lesson. Your writers can then concoct their own commercials or write critiques of ones on TV.)

Ross, Pat. *Gloria and the Super Soaper*. Illus. by Susan Paradis. Little, 1982.
(Gun-loving girl gets to see the real McCoy when she and her father witness a bank robbery.)

Rylant, Cynthia. *When I Was Young in the Mountains*. Illus. by Diane Goode. Dutton, 1982.
(Girl reminisces about her youth. Good for all ages, especially as the starting point for a discussion or writing about childhood memories. For another glimpse of "life in the old days," students can interview parents or grandparents about their childhoods.)

Sachs, Marilyn. *Fleet-Footed Florence*. Illus. by Charles Robinson. Doubleday, 1981.
(Female baseball player becomes a star.)

──────. *Matt's Mitt*. Illus. by Hilary Knight. Doubleday, 1975.

Which dogs make the best librarians?

Hush puppies.

(The greatest catcher of all time owes his skill to his treasured blue baseball mitt.)

Saunders, Susan. *Fish Fry*. Illus. by S.D. Schindler. Viking, 1982.
(Young girl and friend find fish and a live alligator at turn-of-the-century Texas picnic.)

Schertle, Alice. *The April Fool*. Illus. by Emily Arnold McCully. Lothrop, 1981.
("Fool" leads king to his first pair of comfortably fitting shoes.)

Seuss, Dr. *Bartholomew and the Oobleck*. Random, 1949.
(New type of sticky weather confounds the kingdom of Didd.)

――――――. *The 500 Hats of Bartholomew Cubbins*. Vanguard, 1938.
(Boy can't remove his multiplying hats fast enough to suit King Derwin. Design and model your own hats.)

――――――. *The Lorax*. Random, 1971.
(How a land is polluted. In verse.)

Shulevitz, Uri. *The Treasure*. Farrar, 1978.
(Magnificent tale of a man who finds his treasure at home.)

Silverstein, Shel. *The Giving Tree*. Harper, 1964.
(Tree gives up everything to the boy she loves. Good discussion starter on the meaning of friendship and sacrifice.)

Slote, Alfred. *My Robot Buddy*. Illus. by Joel Schick. Lippincott, 1975.
(Boy must save his new human-looking robot friend from nefarious robot-nappers. Chapters.)

Snyder, Carol. *Ike and Mama and the Once-a-Year-Suit*. Illus. by Charles Robinson. Coward, 1978.
(Mama takes the neighborhood children to bargain for clothes in New York City of the 1920s. Look for other "Ike and Mama" books in series. Read in two sittings.)

Steig, William. *The Amazing Bone*. Farrar, 1976.
(Pig's talking bone saves her from a hungry fox.)

――――――. *Dr. DeSoto*. Farrar, 1982.
(Mouse dentist relieves the toothache of an untrustworthy fox.)

Steptoe, John. *Stevie*. Harper, 1969.
(Boy resents his new foster brother until he's gone.)

Talon, Robert. *Zoophabets*. Bobbs, 1971.
(Alliteration with invented creatures. Write your own dictionary, using black paper and pastels for illustrations.)

Thurber, James. *Many Moons*. Illus. by Louis Slobodkin. Harcourt, 1953.
(Princess wants the moon.)

Tripp, Wallace. *Sir Toby Jingle's Beastly Journey*. Coward, 1976.
(Aging knight plans his last great adventure. Good scenes for staging with improvised dialogue.)

Turkle, Brinton. *Do Not Open*. Dutton, 1981.
(Miss Moody finds a mysterious bottle on the beach. Wonderfully scary.)

Udry, Janice May. *Angie*. Illus. by Hilary Knight. Harper, 1971.
(Daily incidents in the life of Angie Brinker, a likable girl who keeps a goose for a pet. Read several chapters a day.)

Van Allsburg, Chris. *The Garden of Abdul Gasazi*. Houghton, 1979.
(Did the ominous magician really turn Fritz the dog into a duck?)

—————. *Jumanji*. Houghton, 1981.
(Two children find a board game that comes to life as they play. Wonderful for creative writing. Have students write the sequel, act it out, and/or design their own board games. A Caldecott winner.)

Viorst, Judith. *Alexander and the Terrible, Horrible, No Good, Very Bad Day*. Illus. by Ray Cruz. Atheneum, 1972.
(Some days are just rotten. Now write about your own lousy ones.)

Waber, Bernard. *Dear Hildegarde*. Houghton, 1980.
(Owl writes "Dear Abby"-ish advice column. Your class can write and answer problem letters of their own.)

—————. *Mice on My Mind*. Houghton, 1977.
(Cat who craves mice is willing to take desperate measures to catch one.)

Warner, Gertrude Chandler. *The Boxcar Children*. Illus. by L. Kate Deal. Whitman, 1950.
(An abandoned train boxcar is home to four orphaned children who run away. Chapters.)

Weil, Lisl. *Owl and Other Scrambles*. Dutton, 1980.
(Word pictures made from the letters in the word. Your students can design some, too.)

White, E.B. *Charlotte's Web*. Illus. by Garth Williams. Harper, 1952.
(Spider saves pig. The classic, perfect for all ages. A chapter a day.)

Wilder, Laura Ingalls. *Little House in the Big Woods*. Illus. by Garth Williams. Harper, 1953.
(First in the autobiographical series about a pioneer family in the 1870s.)

Williams, Jay. *Everyone Knows What a Dragon Looks Like.*
Illus. by Mercer Mayer. Four Winds, 1976.
(Chinese dragon saves a city from ruin, thanks to the only
boy who believes in him.)
—————. *One Big Wish.* Illus. by John O'Brien. Macmil-
lan, 1980.
(Farmer's wishes cause him nothing but trouble.)
—————. *The Question Box.* Illus. by Margot Zemach.
Norton, 1965.
(A girl's curiosity saves her town from invaders.)
Yashima, Taro. *Crow Boy.* Viking, 1955.
(Japanese tale of an outcast boy who proves his value to
his classmates. Insightful and a fine stimulus for a class
discussion.)
Zemach, Harve. *The Judge.* Illus. by Margot Zemach. Farrar,
1969.
(Pompous judge won't believe his prisoners' tales of an
approaching monster. In rhyme and great to act out.)
Zolotow, Charlotte. *Someday.* Illus. by Arnold Lobel. Harper,
1965.
(One girl's wishful thinking. Your children can write their
own wishes.)

Read-Aloud Fiction
for Grades 3–4

Anderson, Margaret. *The Brain on Quartz Mountain*. Illus. by Charles Robinson. Knopf, 1982.
(David helps an eccentric professor educate a growing chicken brain.)

Atwater, Richard and Florence. *Mr. Popper's Penguins*. Illus. by Robert Lawson. Little, 1938.
(Placid house painter receives a live penguin as a gift from a South Pole explorer.)

Bacon, Peggy. *The Magic Touch*. Little, 1968.
(Four children try out a recipe book of magic spells and are transformed into cats, dogs, rabbits, and birds.)

Blume, Judy. *Tales of a Fourth Grade Nothing*. Illus. by Roy Doty. Dutton, 1972.
(Peter must learn to cope with his incorrigible little brother, Fudgie.)

Burnett, Frances Hodgson. *Sara Crewe: Or What Happened at Miss Minchin's*. Illus. by Margot Tomes. Putnam, 1981.
(Orphaned girl becomes a servant at her former school in this shorter original version of the Victorian classic, *The Little Princess*.)

Byars, Betsy. *The Midnight Fox*. Illus. by Ann Grifalconi. Viking, 1968.
(City boy spends a memorable summer on his aunt and uncle's farm.)

——————. *The Winged Colt of Casa Mia*. Illus. by Richard Cuffari. Viking, 1973.
(Former stuntman and his bookish nephew attempt to train a newborn horse that can fly.)

Cleary, Beverly. *The Mouse and the Motorcycle*. Illus. by Louis Darling. Morrow, 1965.
(Boy meets a remarkable mouse named Ralph at a mountain hotel. Your students will want to read the 1970 sequel, *Runaway Ralph*.)

——————. *Ralph S. Mouse*. Illus. by Paul O. Zelinsky. Morrow, 1982.
(Motorcycle-riding mouse goes to school.)

——————. *Ramona Quimby, Age 8*. Illus. by Alan Tiegreen. Morrow, 1981.
(Former pest hits third grade. Not to be missed!)

Clifford, Sandy. *The Roquefort Gang*. Houghton, 1981.
(To babysitter Nicole's horror, her mouse twin charges disappear into the dreaded Wild-berry Lot.)

Clymer, Eleanor. *My Brother Stevie.* Holt, 1967.
(Annie feels responsible for her brother's misbehavior.)

Cone, Molly. *Mishmash.* Illus. by Leonard Shortall. Houghton, 1962.
(Pete gets a troublemaking pet dog who acts almost human. First in a series.)

Conford, Ellen. *Me and the Terrible Two.* Illus. by Charles Carroll. Little, 1974.
(When Dorrie's best friend moves away, she is saddled with obnoxious twin boys as neighbors.)

Corbett, Scott. *The Lemonade Trick.* Illus. by Paul Galdone. Little, 1960.
(First in a series about a boy's chemistry set that always produces unexpected and amusing results.)

——————. *The Limerick Trick.* Illus. by Paul Galdone. Little, 1964.
(Kirby uses his magic chemistry set to try to win the bicycle prize for the school poetry contest.)

——————. *The Turnabout Trick.* Illus. by Paul Galdone. Little, 1964.
(Cat becomes dog-like and vice versa as Kirby puts his chemistry set to use.)

Dahl, Roald. *The BFG.* Illus. by Quentin Blake. Farrar, 1982.
(Befriended by the Big Friendly Giant who has kidnapped her, young orphan Sophie enlists his help in preventing nine repulsive human-guzzling giants from eating innocent children. The BFG is a language mangler of the highest order, making each of his speeches an event to be savored.)

——————. *Charlie and the Chocolate Factory.* Illus. by Joseph Schindelman. Knopf, 1964.
(Only the five children who find the gold ticket in their candy bars will win a trip through Mr. Wonka's fabulous factory.)

——————. *James and the Giant Peach.* Illus. by Nancy Ekholm Burkert. Knopf, 1961.
(Orphan boy and giant insect friends travel over the ocean in one grand adventure.)

DeJong, Meindert. *Hurry Home, Candy.* Illus. by Maurice Sendak. Harper, 1953.
(Nameless stray dog finds human companionship in his travels.)

Drury, Roger W. *The Finches' Fabulous Furnace.* Illus. by Erik Blegvad. Little, 1971.
(There's a volcano in their cellar, and it's growing!)

Edwards, Julie. *The Last of the Really Great Whangdoodles.* Harper, 1974.
(Professor instructs three children in their search for this elusive animal in the kingdom of Whangdoodleland.)
Farley, Walter. *The Black Stallion.* Random, 1941.
(Boy and horse survive a shipwreck and more.)
Fleischman, Sid. *McBroom Tells the Truth.* Illus. by Kurt Werth. Little, 1966. (Tall tale of a farmer's eleven children and their fabulous one-acre farm. Get students exaggerating by writing their own whoppers. Look for other "McBroom" books in the series, newly released by Little, Brown and illustrated by Walter Lorraine.)

Illustration by Ron Barrett from ANIMALS SHOULD DEFINITELY NOT WEAR CLOTHING. Text copyright © 1970 by Judith Barrett. Illustrations copyright © 1970 by Ron Barrett. Reproduced by permission of Atheneum Publishers.

Garfield, James B. *Follow My Leader*. Illus. by Robert Greiner. Viking, 1957.
(After being blinded by a firecracker, Jimmy must learn to adjust to his handicap.)

Giff, Patricia Reilly. *Left-Handed Shortstop*. Illus. by Leslie Morrill. Delacorte, 1980.
(When the fifth grade challenges the fourth to a baseball game, Walter looks for a way out.)

Gwynne, Fred. *A Chocolate Moose for Dinner*. Dutton, 1976.
(Picture book of figures of speech, taken literally. Illustrate your own.)

—————. *The King Who Rained*. Dutton, 1970.
(More marvelously misunderstood figures of speech.)

Harding, Lee. *The Fallen Spaceman*. Illus. by John and Ian Schoenherr. Harper, 1980.
(Alien is trapped on Earth when the main spaceship leaves him behind by mistake.)

Hart, Carole. *Delilah*. Illus. by Edward Frascino. Harper, 1973.
(Short episodes in the ninth year of a spunky girl.)

Heide, Florence Parry. *The Shrinking of Treehorn*. Illus. by Edward Gorey. Holiday, 1971.
(No one seems to notice that he's getting smaller.)

Henry, Marguerite. *Misty of Chincoteague*. Illus. by Wesley Dennis. Rand, 1947.
(Horse story involving two children who help to capture and tame a wild mare and her colt.)

Hildick, E.W. *The Case of the Condemned Cat*. Illus. by Lisl Weil. Macmillan, 1975.
(One of the tongue-in-cheek series about the McGurk Organization, a neighborhood group of kid detectives. Read just one and your students will be hooked.)

Hooks, William H. *Mean Jake and the Devils*. Illus. by Dirk Zimmer. Dial, 1981.
(Three Halloween-time tales, taken from U.S. folklore.)

Hughes, Ted. *The Iron Giant: A Story in Five Nights*. Illus. by Robert Nadler. Harper, 1968.
(Metal-devouring giant settles contentedly in a junkyard until a space-bat-angel-dragon monster threatens Earth's existence. Read the five chapters over the course of one thrilling week.)

Ipcar, Dahlov. *I Love My Anteater with an A*. Knopf, 1964.
(Animal alliteration picture book makes a great dictionary and writing activity.)

Kennedy, Richard. *The Leprechaun's Story*. Illus. by Marcia Sewell. Dutton, 1979.
(Leprechaun tricks a gullible man out of his pot of gold in this witty picture book.)

————. *The Lost Kingdom of Karnica*. Illus. by Uri Shulevitz. Scribner, 1979.
(Greedy king is willing to destroy his entire kingdom to dig up a giant precious stone.)

————. *The Rise and Fall of Ben Gizzard*. Illus. by Marcia Sewell. Little, 1978.
(Old West bad guy finally gets his due.)

Levy, Elizabeth. *Lizzie Lies a Lot*. Illus. by John Wallner. Delacorte, 1976.
(The lies that Lizzie tells to her friends, parents, and grandmother finally catch up with her.)

Lewis, C.S. *The Lion, the Witch and the Wardrobe*. Illus. by Pauline Baynes. Macmillan, 1950.
(Classic fantasy of four children who discover the enchanted winter-locked land of Narnia. First book in a series of seven.)

Lindgren, Astrid. *Pippi Longstocking*. Illus. by Louis S. Glanzman. Viking, 1950.
(Zany eccentricities of red-haired Swedish girl. First of a series.)

Manes, Steven. *Be a Perfect Person in Just Three Days!* Illus. by Tom Huffman. Clarion, 1982.
(Milo finds a strange book which gives instructions.)

McGraw, Eloise Jarvis. *Joel and the Great Merlini*. Illus. by Jim Arnosky. Pantheon, 1979.
(Boy performs stupendous magic tricks thanks to the help of an overzealous wizard.)

Miles, Betty. *The Secret Life of the Underwear Champ*. Illus. by Dan Jones. Knopf, 1981.
(Making TV commercials is not all fun, especially when they interfere with Little League practice.)

Moskin, Marietta. *The Day of the Blizzard*. Illus. by Stephen Gammell. Coward, 1978.
(Katie ventures out during the Great Blizzard of 1888 in New York City.)

Mowat, Farley. *Owls in the Family*. Illus. by Robert Frankenberg. Little, 1961.
(Canadian author describes the unusual wild pets he tamed as a boy.)

Oakley, Graham. *The Church Mouse*. Atheneum, 1972.

(First of a marvelously detailed series about Sampson the cat and his mouse charges. Make sure everyone sits up close so that no one will miss any of the mouse antics.)

Ormondroyd, Edward. *David and the Phoenix*. Illus. by Joan Raysor. Follett, 1957.
(Boy meets mythical bird who flies him all around the world.)

Park, Barbara. *Operation: Dump the Chump*. Knopf, 1982.
(Oscar thinks up a foolproof plan to get rid of his pesty younger brother.)

Peet, Bill. *The Wump World*. Houghton, 1970.
(Peaceful Wump planet is invaded by the Pollutians from the planet Pollutus. Picture book ties in well to any ecology lesson.)

Phelan, Terry Wolfe. *The Week Mom Unplugged the TVs*. Illus. by Joel Schick. Four Winds, 1979.
(Good kick-off for no-TV week, or as a means to get students thinking about alternatives to the idiot box.)

Pinkwater, Daniel Manus. *Fat Men from Space*. Dodd, 1977.
(Aliens plan to invade Earth, rob it of all its junk food, and make Earthlings their slaves.)

——————. *The Hoboken Chicken Emergency*. Prentice, 1977.
(Arthur's new six-foot, 266-pound pet chicken, Henrietta, escapes. A very funny Thanksgiving saga.)

——————. *The Magic Moscow*. Four Winds, 1980.
(Excitable ice cream parlor owner buys Edward, an Alaskan malamute that is supposedly the grandson of a TV wonderdog.)

Porter, David Lord. *Help! Let Me Out*. Illus. by David Macaulay. Houghton, 1982.
(When Hugo learns to throw his voice, it leaves him speechless, preferring to go off on its own. Read in one sitting.)

Reit, Seymour. *Benvenuto*. Illus. by Will Winslow. Addison, 1974.
(Paolo finds a baby dragon at summer camp and takes it home to his New York City apartment.)

Richler, Mordecai. *Jacob Two-Two Meets the Hooded Fang*. Illus. by Fritz Wegner. Knopf, 1975.
(Sent to Slimer's Isle dungeon for being a smart alecky kid, Jacob thwarts the rotten kid-hating villain who runs the prison.)

Rockwell, Thomas. *How To Eat Fried Worms*. Illus. by Emily

McCully. Watts, 1973.
(A fifty-dollar worm-eating bet is accepted by Billy, who claims he can eat anything. Hilarious, but not before lunch.)

Sachar, Louis. *Sideways Stories from Wayside School.* Illus. by Dennis Hockerman. Follett, 1978.
(Wacky tales from the top floor classroom in a school that is thirty stories high.)

Selden, George. *Chester Cricket's Pigeon Ride.* Illus. by Garth Williams. Farrar, 1981.

Illustration from A BEAR CALLED PADDINGTON by Michael Bond, illustrated by Peggy Fortnum. Copyright © 1958 by Michael Bond. Reproduced by permission of Houghton Mifflin Company.

(A bird's-eye view of New York City.)

—————. *The Cricket in Times Square*. Illus. by Garth Williams. Farrar, 1960.
(Musical cricket from Connecticut is befriended by a cat, a mouse, and a boy in the 42nd Street subway station of New York City.)

—————. *Harry Cat's Pet Puppy*. Illus. by Garth Williams. Farrar, 1974.
(Raising a puppy in a subway station is not an easy task for Harry Cat and Tucker Mouse in this sequel to *The Cricket in Times Square*.)

Shura, Mary Francis. *Chester*. Illus. by Susan Swan. Dodd, 1980.
(New neighbor has the most freckles, siblings, and pets on the whole block.)

Slobodkin, Louis. *The Space Ship Under the Apple Tree*. Collier, 1952.
(Science fiction tale of an Earth boy who befriends a little man from the planet Martinea.)

Slote, Alfred. *My Trip to Alpha I*. Illus. by Harold Berson. Lippincott, 1978.
(Jack uncovers a sinister plot when he visits his aunt on another planet.)

Smith, Robert Kimmell. *Chocolate Fever*. Illus. by Gioia Fiammenghi. Coward, 1972.
(Henry Green's chocolate fetish goes too far. Also a 1978 Dell paperback.)

Sobol, Donald J. *Encyclopedia Brown, Boy Detective*. Illus. by Leonard Shortall. Nelson, 1963.
(America's "Sherlock Holmes in sneakers" solves his first ten mysteries. Try any in the series; all are guaranteed to test your powers of deductive reasoning.)

Steig, William. *Caleb and Kate*. Farrar, 1977.
(Unbeknown to his wife, carpenter is turned into a dog by a witch. A picture book that appeals to older children especially.)

Stolz, Mary. *The Bully of Barkham Street*. Illus. by Leonard Shortall. Harper, 1963.
(Psychology of a bully. Your students may want to read *A Dog on Barkham Street*, 1960, for the same story, but from the bully's victim's point of view.)

—————. *Cat Walk*. Illus. by Erik Blegvad. Harper, 1983.
(Barn cat who yearns for a human-given name and a real home ends up with both.)

Storr, Càtherine. *Clever Polly and the Stupid Wolf.* Illus. by Marjorie-Ann Watts. Faber, 1979.
(Polly continues to outwit the wolf who wants to make her his supper.)

Titus, Eve. *Basil of Baker Street.* Illus. by Paul Galdone. McGraw, 1958.
(Mouse detective of Sherlock Holmes's basement solves the toughest case of his career. First of a series.)

Tripp, Wallace. *My Uncle Podger.* Little, 1975.
(Self-important rabbit hangs a picture. Using judicious editing, narrate the action and have your students enact Uncle Podger's bumbling attempts.)

Van Allsburg, Chris. *The Wreck of the Zephyr.* Houghton, 1983.
(Boy meets an old sailor who tells him about an airborne sailboat. A picture book for credulous children.)

Van de Wetering, Janwillem. *Hugh Pine.* Illus. by Lynn Munsinger. Houghton, 1980.
(Maine porcupine who learns to walk and talk must save his fellow porcupines from the cars that can kill them.)

Van Leeuwen, Jean. *The Great Cheese Conspiracy.* Illus. by Imero Gobbato. Random, 1969.
(Three daring mice plot a cheese store heist. Also a 1976 Dell paperback.)

————. *The Great Christmas Kidnapping Caper.* Illus. by Steven Kellogg. Dial, 1975.
(After the Macy's department store Santa disappears, three tough mice come to the rescue. Sequel to *The Great Cheese Conspiracy.*)

Wagner, Jane. *J.T.* Photos. by Gordon Parks, Jr. Dell, 1969 (pbk. only).
(Lonely city boy adopts a stray cat and nurses it back to health.)

Wetterer, Margaret. *The Giant's Apprentice.* Illus. by Elise Primavera. Atheneum, 1982.
(Blacksmith's apprentice is kidnapped by a giant on Halloween night. Also good to read on St. Patrick's Day.)

White, Anne Hitchcock. *Junket: The Dog Who Liked Everything "Just So."* Illus. by Robert McCloskey. Viking, 1955.
(Irrepressible terrier befriends the new family that moves to his farm.)

White, E.B. *Stuart Little.* Illus. by Garth Williams. Harper, 1945.
(In spite of his diminutive size, mouse born to a human family thrives in New York City.)

Wilder, Laura Ingalls. *Farmer Boy*. Illus. by Garth Williams. Harper, 1953.
(About the childhood of Laura Ingalls Wilder's husband, Almanzo.)

Wilson, Gahan. *Harry the Fat Bear Spy*. Scribner, 1973.
(Who is turning Bearmania's famous macaroons green?)

Wolkoff, Judie. *Wally*. Bradbury, 1977.
(Contrary to explicit instructions from his mother, Michael agrees to reptile-sit his friend's pet chuckwalla.)

Zhitkov, Boris. *How I Hunted the Little Fellows*. Illus. by Paul O. Zelinsky. Dodd, 1979.
(Russian boy's imagination gets the better of him when he is forbidden to touch his grandmother's model steamship. Good dramatic scenes for narrative pantomime, encompassing the character's emotional development. Students can then tell or write the worst things *they* ever did.)

Illustration from THE CHAMPION OF MERRIMACK COUNTY by Roger W. Drury. Copyright © 1976 by Roger W. Drury. Illustrations by Fritz Wegner. Reproduced by permission of Little, Brown and Company.

Read-Aloud Fiction
for Grades 4–5

Alexander, Lloyd. *The Cat Who Wished To Be a Man*. Dutton, 1973.
(An enchanter grants cat Lionel's wish, with hilarious results.)

Arthur, Robert. *The Secret of Terror Castle*. Illus. by Harry Kane. Random, 1964.
(Suspenseful mystery of a haunted mansion. First in the "Three Investigators" series, which can prove an addiction for suspense-lovers.)

Baldwin, Ann Norris. *A Little Time*. Viking, 1978.
(Downs Syndrome-afflicted little brother causes Ginny conflicting emotions of love and resentment.)

Beatty, Jerome. *Matthew Looney's Invasion of the Earth*. Illus. by Gahan Wilson. Scott, 1965.
(Moon boy joins earth-bound expedition searching for intelligent life. One of a series about the Looney family. Also look for "Maria Looney" books about Matthew's younger sister.)

Bellairs, John. *The House with a Clock in Its Walls*. Illus. by Edward Gorey. Dial, 1973.
(After orphaned Lewis moves into Uncle Jonathan's mansion, they investigate the constant and insidious ticking within the walls. If the class insists, follow up with the 1975 sequel, *The Figure in the Shadows*.)

Blume, Judy. *Superfudge*. Dutton, 1980.
(A new baby named Tootsie adds to the mayhem when the Hatcher family moves from New York City to Princeton, New Jersey. Hilarious sequel to *Tales of a Fourth Grade Nothing*.)

Bond, Michael. *A Bear Called Paddington*. Illus. by Peggy Fortnum. Houghton, 1960.
(First in a long series about that well-meaning but trouble-causing English bear from darkest Peru. Filled with Briticisms and straight-faced slapstick.)

Brady, Esther Wood. *Toliver's Secret*. Illus. by Richard Cuffari. Crown, 1976.
(Disguised as a boy, Ellen must deliver a message hidden in a loaf of bread to General Washington.)

Brenner, Barbara. *A Year in the Life of Rosie Bernard*. Illus. by Joan Sandin. Harper, 1971.
(Ten-year-old Rosie spends 1932 with her cousins and

grandparents, living through "hard times" with her usual aplomb.)

Brink, Carol Ryrie. *The Bad Times of Irma Baumlein*. Illus. by Trina Schart Hyman. Macmillan, 1972.
(When Irma tells a classmate that she owns the largest doll in the world, her lie backfires, leading to more deception and even to stealing.)

──────. *Caddie Woodlawn*. Illus. by Kate Seredy. Macmillan, 1935.
(Based on the stories of the author's grandmother as a twelve year old in a Wisconsin frontier family. A Newbery winner.)

Brittain, Bill. *All the Money in the World*. Illus. by Charles Robinson. Harper, 1979.
(Rufus helps out a leprechaun who grants him three wishes. Have your class decide what *their* wishes would have been and how they might have backfired.)

Burch, Robert. *Ida Early Comes over the Mountain*. Viking, 1980.
(Exuberant young new housekeeper cares for the four motherless Sutton children in rural Georgia during the Depression.)

Butterworth, Oliver. *The Enormous Egg*. Illus. by Louis Darling. Little, 1956.
(Chicken hatches a dinosaur egg, giving farmboy Nate his own pet triceratops.)

Byars, Betsy. *The 18th Emergency*. Illus. by Robert Grossman. Viking, 1973.
(Weakling known as "Mouse" awaits a beating from Marv Hammerman, the school's biggest bully.)

Chase, Mary. *Loretta Mason Potts*. Illus. by Harold Berson. Lippincott, 1958.
(After Colin's mysterious, rotten older sister comes home for the first time in years, he sets out to find the fantastic secret of the hill that holds such a powerful influence over her. An entertaining fantasy.)

Cohen, Barbara. *Thank You, Jackie Robinson*. Illus. by Richard Cuffari. Lothrop, 1974.
(New Jersey boy baseball nut becomes best friends with a sixty-year-old black man who shares his passion for the game.)

Conford, Ellen. *The Revenge of the Incredible Dr. Rancid and His Youthful Assistant, Jeffrey*. Little, 1980.
(Even the skinniest boy in the sixth grade can become a superhero in his own imagination.)

Corbett, Scott. *Cop's Kid*. Illus. by Jo Polseno. Little, 1968.
(Two brothers trail a stick-up man after he deliberately
burns the younger one with his cigarette.)

—————. *The Donkey Planet*. Illus. by Troy Howell. Dutton, 1979.
(Two Earth scientists are transformed into a boy and a
donkey when they are sent to Vanaris on a dangerous mission.)

—————. *The Red Room Riddle*. Illus. by Geff Gerlach.
Little, 1972.
(Two boys search for ghosts one memorable but terrifying
Halloween night.)

Coren, Alan. *Railroad Arthur*. Illus. by John Astrop. Little,
1977.
(Tongue-in-cheek tale of a ten-year-old boy, under suspicion of robbing trains, who endeavors to find the real villains. One of a series about Arthur.)

Coville, Bruce. *The Monster's Ring*. Illus. by Katherine
Coville. Pantheon, 1982.
(Russell obtains a magic ring with terrifying powers. Students can act out his horrifying transformation in narrative
pantomime.)

De Jong, Meindert. *The Wheel on the School*. Illus. by Maurice Sendak. Harper, 1954.
(Dutch girl and her friends lure the storks back to their
town. A Newbery winner.)

Drury, Roger W. *The Champion of Merrimack County*. Illus.
by Fritz Wegner. Little, 1976.
(Mouse cyclist hurts his tail and his bicycle when he shows
off while riding around Mr. Berryfield's antique bathtub.)

Fitzgerald, John D. *The Great Brain*. Illus. by Mercer Mayer.
Dial, 1967.
(Uproarious autobiographical tales by the brother of a
money-hungry, conniving young genius. First in a series of
seven "Great Brain" books.)

Fleischman, Sid. *By the Great Horn Spoon*. Illus. by Eric von
Schmidt. Little, 1963.
(Young Jack Flagg and his faultless butler, Praiseworthy,
hunt for gold in old California.)

—————. *Humbug Mountain*. Illus. by Eric von Schmidt.
Little, 1978.
(Wandering newspaperman and family end up in a ghost
town with two Old West villains.)

Fleming, Susan. *Trapped on the Golden Flyer*. Illus. by Alex

Stein. Westminster, 1978.
(A dangerous blizzard interrupts Paul's California-bound train ride.)

Garrigue, Sheila. *Between Friends.* Bradbury, 1978.
(Jill's loyalty is tested by her new friendship with Dede, a retarded girl.)

George, Jean Craighead. *My Side of the Mountain.* Dutton, 1967.
(Sam learns to survive by his wits when he camps out in his own mountain treehouse.)

Giff, Patricia Reilly. *The Winter Worm Business.* Illus. by Leslie Morrill. Delacorte, 1981.
(Leroy's most unfavorite cousin moves to town.)

Gilson, Jamie. *Dial Leroi Rupert, DJ.* Illus. by John Wallner. Lothrop, 1979.
(Three boys in trouble need to earn thirty dollars fast, before their parents find out what they've done to Dr. Scharff's window.)

――――――――. *Harvey the Beer Can King.* Illus. by John Wallner. Lothrop, 1978.
(Harvey hopes his can collection will help him win the Superkid Contest.)

Gipson, Fred. *Old Yeller.* Illus. by Carl Burger. Harper, 1956.
(Poignant 1860s Texas tale of a boy and the mangy old stray who comes to stay.)

Girion, Barbara. *Misty and Me.* Scribner, 1979.
(Kim finds a dog-sitter for the new puppy she is not supposed to have.)

Gormley, Beatrice. *Fifth Grade Magic.* Illus. by Emily Arnold McCully. Dutton, 1982.
(When Gretchen fails to get a part in the fifth grade play, a bumbling young fairy godmother tries to rectify the situation.)

――――――――. *Mail-Order Wings.* Illus. by Emily Arnold McCully. Dutton, 1981.
(Andrea gets wings that really work. After reading this, a flying contest will be in order.)

Gould, Marilyn. *Golden Daffodils.* Addison, 1982.
(Afflicted since birth with cerebral palsy, Janice adapts to being mainstreamed into a regular fifth grade class.)

Greene, Bette. *Philip Hall Likes Me. I Reckon, Maybe.* Illus. by Charles Lilly. Dial, 1974.
(Rural Arkansas girl's first crush on the #1 student in her class may be the reason she is #2.)

Greenwald, Sheila. *The Atrocious Two*. Houghton, 1978.
(Two obnoxious children become reformed when they are sent to spend the summer with tough Aunt Tessie.)

Haynes, Betsy. *The Ghost of the Gravestone Hearth*. Nelson, 1977.
(Charlie meets up with a real pirate ghost who needs help in locating a buried chest of gold.)

Herman, Charlotte. *Our Snowman Had Olive Eyes*. Dutton, 1977.
(The year Sheila's seventy-nine-year-old grandmother moves in, they share a bedroom and a special closeness.)

Hicks, Clifford B. *Alvin's Swap Shop*. Illus. by Bill Sokol. Holt, 1976.
(How to swap an ant for more valuable items. Another in the humorous "Alvin Fernald" mystery and adventure series.)

————. *Peter Potts*. Dutton, 1971. Avon, 1979 (pbk.).
(Accident-prone boy and his grand schemes. Read April Fool's Day chapter *after* April Fool's Day, if you know what's good for you!)

Hildick, E.W. *McGurk Gets Good and Mad*. Illus. by Lisl Weil. Macmillan, 1982.
(Who is trying to sabotage the McGurk Organization's First Annual Open House? Another delightful mystery in this on-going series.)

Holland, Barbara. *Prisoners at the Kitchen Table*. Houghton, 1979.
(Two children are kidnapped and held captive in a remote farmhouse.)

Holman, Felice. *The Blackmail Machine*. Illus. by Victoria de Larrea. Macmillan, 1968.
(Adding a propeller to a treehouse enables it to fly, giving four children a chance to have their voices heard by the town authorities.)

Howe, Deborah and James. *Bunnicula*. Illus. by Alan Daniel. Atheneum, 1979.
(Is the Monroe family's new pet really a vampire bunny? A wild tale of exorcism gone amok, as related by Harold, the family dog.)

Howe, James. *Howliday Inn*. Illus. by Lynn Munsinger. Atheneum, 1982.
(The Monroe family's cat and dog investigate possible werewolves when they are boarded at a kennel for a week. Sequel to *Bunnicula*.)

Keller, Beverly. *The Genuine, Ingenious, Thrift Shop Genie, Clarissa Mae Bean and Me.* Illus. by Raymond Davidson. Coward, 1977.
(Marcie is friends with the weirdest girl in school. An off-beat comedy.)

Konigsburg, E.L. *From the Mixed-Up Files of Mrs. Basil E. Frankweiler.* Atheneum, 1967.
(Claudia and her little brother run away to the Metropolitan Museum of Art in New York City. A Newbery Award winner.)

Krensky, Stephen. *The Dragon Circle.* Illus. by A. Delaney. Atheneum, 1977.
(The unexpected appearance of dragons causes the Wynd family's usual magic spells to go awry.)

Lane, Carolyn. *Echoes in an Empty Room.* Holt, 1980.
(Tales of the supernatural.)

Levitin, Sonia. *Jason and the Money Tree.* Illus. by Pat Grant Porter. Harcourt, 1974.
(Boy grows a plant from a ten-dollar bill in his back yard.)

Lewis, C.S. *The Magician's Nephew.* Illus. by Pauline Baynes. Macmillan, 1955.
(How Aslan, the noble lion, created the land of Narnia, and about the English children who find themselves there. One of seven in the "Chronicles of Narnia" that began with *The Lion, the Witch and the Wardrobe.*)

Little, Jean. *Home from Far.* Illus. by Jerry Lazare. Little, 1965.
(Six months after her twin brother has died in an auto accident, Jenny must adjust to the new foster brother and sister that her parents take in.)

Masterman-Smith, Virginia. *The Treasure Trap.* Illus. by Roseanne Litzinger. Four Winds, 1979.
(Children dig up yard in search for a millionaire's long-lost treasure.)

McCloskey, Robert. *Homer Price.* Viking, 1943.
(Unflappable Ohio boy contends with a pet skunk, robbers, an overloaded doughnut machine, and more.)

McMurtry, Stan. *The Bunjee Venture.* Scholastic, 1977 (pbk. only).
(After Mr. Winsborrow and his flimsy homemade time machine disappear from the family garage, his two children construct a sturdier model and travel back to prehistoric times to find him.)

Meyers, Susan. *P.J. Clover, Private Eye: The Case of the*

Stolen Laundry. Messner, 1981.
(Young girl turns detective.)

Miles, Miska. *Annie and the Old One*. Illus. by Peter Parnall. Little, 1971.
(Indian girl fears and tries to prevent her grandmother's death.)

Naylor, Phyllis Reynolds. *Witch's Sister*. Illus. by Gail Owens. Atheneum, 1975.
(Lynn and her friend Mouse join forces against Mrs. Tuggle, whom they suspect of being a witch. First in a chilling trilogy, ending with *Witch Water*, 1977, and *The Witch Herself*, 1978.)

Nostlinger, Christine. *Konrad*. Illus. by Carol Nicklaus. Watts, 1977.
(Factory-produced canned kid is delivered by mistake to Mrs. Bartolotti, an eccentric weaver.)

Park, Barbara. *Skinnybones*. Knopf, 1982.
(A wild sense of humor saves Little League's worst player.)

Peck, Robert Newton. *Soup and Me*. Illus. by Charles Lilly. Knopf, 1975.
(Two best friends are always in trouble. Look for other amusing titles in the autobiographical "Soup" series.)

Pfeffer, Susan Beth. *Kid Power*. Illus. by Leigh Grant. Watts, 1977.
(Janie starts an odd-jobs agency to earn money for her new bike.)

Pinkwater, Daniel Manus. *The Slaves of Spiegel: A Magic Moscow Story*. Four Winds, 1982.
(Fat men from the planet Spiegel hold an intergalactic junk food cook-off.)

—————. *Yobgorgle: Mystery Monster of Lake Ontario*. Houghton, 1979.
(Eugene and his Uncle Mel join in the search for the newest creature since Nessie.)

Pinkwater, Manus. *Lizard Music*. Dodd, 1976.
(Home alone with both parents and sister away on vacation, Victor starts seeing lizards everywhere. For Walter Cronkite fans.)

Robinson, Barbara. *The Best Christmas Pageant Ever*. Illus. by Judith Gwyn Brown. Harper, 1972.
(The horrible Herdman kids steal all the main parts in the church Christmas play.)

Rosenbloom, Joseph. *Maximilian, You're the Greatest*. Nelson, 1980.

(Punning boy detective solves sixteen cases. In the "Encyclopedia Brown" vein.)

Rounds, Glenn. *Mr. Yowder and the Lion Roar Capsules.* Holiday, 1976.
(Peripatetic sign painter is given a broken-down lion in payment for his work. Dry, understated humor.)

——————. *Mr. Yowder and the Train Robbers.* Holiday, 1981.
(Sign painter foils dangerous outlaws with the help of co-operative rattlesnakes. Act out scene with outlaws, using improvised dialogue.)

Roy, Ron. *Nightmare Island.* Illus. by Robert MacLean. Dutton, 1981.
(Two brothers are trapped by fire on their camping trip to a tiny Maine island.)

Sachs, Marilyn. *Veronica Ganz.* Illus. by Louis Glanzman. Doubleday, 1968.
(A girl bully meets her match in Peter Wedermeyer, the shrimpy new boy in her class.)

Shura, Mary Francis. *Mister Wolf and Me.* Illus. by Konrad Hack. Dodd, 1979.
(Miles's pet German shepherd is accused of killing sheep.)

Simon, Seymour. *Einstein Anderson, Science Sleuth.* Illus. by Fred Winkowski. Viking, 1980.
(First of an "Encyclopedia Brown"–like series of science-based mysteries your students will delight in solving.)

Sleator, William. *Among the Dolls.* Illus. by Trina Schart Hyman. Dutton, 1975.
(Dolls imprison Vicky in her own dollhouse to retaliate for her abuse of them.)

Slote, Alfred. *Hang Tough, Paul Mather.* Lippincott, 1973.
(Baseball lover gets leukemia. No one writes better children's baseball novels; look for his other titles for your student fans.)

Sperry, Armstrong. *Call It Courage.* Macmillan, 1940.
(Polynesian chief's son must overcome his fear of the sea to become accepted. A Newbery winner.)

Stearns, Pamela. *Into the Painted Bear Lair.* Illus. by Ann Strugnell. Houghton, 1976.
(After Gregory finds himself in a hungry bear's sitting room, he enlists the help of a female knight to get him home again.)

Steig, William. *Abel's Island.* Farrar, 1976.
(Gentleman mouse is stranded on an island apart from his beloved wife, Amanda, and must learn to fend for himself.)

Stonely, Jack. *Scruffy*. Random, 1979.
(Abandoned puppy survives to become the most famous dog in England.)

Sutton, Jane. *Me and the Weirdos*. Illus. by Sandy Kossin. Houghton, 1981.
(Cindy Krinkle decides to un-weird her eccentric family, and learns to accept their zany ways in the process.)

Talbot, Charlene Joy. *An Orphan for Nebraska*. Atheneum, 1979.
(Homeless Irish immigrant boy is taken in by a newspaper-man in 1872.)

Van Leeuwen, Jean. *The Great Rescue Operation*. Illus. by Margot Apple. Dial, 1982.
(Mouse missing from Macy's toy department is hunted by his two mouse pals. Whimsical sequel to *The Great Christmas Kidnapping Caper*.)

White, Anne Hitchcock. *A Dog Called Scholar*. Illus. by Lillian Obligado. Viking, 1963.
(In spite of his pedigree, the Tuckers's new golden retriever pup is full of mischief.)

White, E.B. *The Trumpet of the Swan*. Illus. by Edward Frascino. Harper, 1970.
(Trumpeter swan born without a voice finds a unique way to make himself heard.)

Williams, Jay. *The Magic Grandfather*. Illus. by Gail Owens. Four Winds, 1979.
(While practicing a magic trick, Sam accidentally causes his sorcerer grandfather to disappear.)

Williams, Jay, and Abrashkin, Raymond. *Danny Dunn and the Homework Machine*. Illus. by Ezra Jack Keats. McGraw, 1958.
(Although written long before the advent of the home computer, this is a tale your homework-haters will relish.)

————. *Danny Dunn, Time Traveler*. Illus. by Owen Kampen. McGraw, 1963.
(Danny and his cohorts are stranded in colonial times when he accidentally breaks Professor Bullfinch's time machine. Look for other entertaining science-oriented adventures in the "Danny Dunn" series.)

Read-Aloud Fiction
for Grades 5—6

Alexander, Lloyd. *The Book of Three.* Holt, 1964.
(Taran, an enchanter's assistant pig-keeper, dreams of glory and adventure. First of five in the riveting "Prydain Chronicles" fantasy.)
—————. *The First Two Lives of Lukas-Kasha.* Dutton, 1978.
(Ne'er-do-well becomes king of an unknown land, thanks to his encounter with a marketplace conjurer.)
—————. *The Town Cats and Other Tales.* Illus. by Laszlo Kubinyi. Dutton, 1977.
(Eight folktale-like stories about shrewd felines.)
—————. *The Wizard in the Tree.* Illus. by Laszlo Kubinyi. Dutton, 1975.
(Mallory, servant girl at the local inn, helps an enchanter regain his powers.)
Ames, Mildred. *Is There Life on a Plastic Planet?* Dutton, 1975.
(Hollis switches places with her double—a life-sized doll.)
Angell, Judie. *The Buffalo Nickel Blues Band.* Bradbury, 1982.
(Junior high schoolers make music and money.)
Armstrong, William. *Sounder.* Illus. by James Barkley. Harper, 1969.
(Poor black sharecropper is jailed for stealing a ham, leaving behind his family and their wounded hound. A Newbery Award book.)
Avi. *Night Journeys.* Pantheon, 1979.
(Peter York, the orphaned ward of a Quaker justice of the peace, assists two young indentured servants in their escape from New Jersey into Pennsylvania in 1767.)
—————. *Shadrach's Crossing.* Pantheon, 1983.
(Liquor smugglers have terrorized the island where twelve-year-old Shad lives, and he skirts danger, intent on bringing the crooks to justice. A thrilling Depression-era story.)
Babbit, Natalie. *The Devil's Storybook.* Farrar, 1974.
(Ten entertaining short stories about the ever-scheming, often bested Devil.)
—————. *The Eyes of the Amaryllis.* Farrar, 1977.
(A mystical, disturbing tale of the intense old woman, whose husband drowned with his ship decades before, and

her granddaughter who helps her search the shore for a sign from him.)

—————, *The Search for Delicious*. Ariel, 1969.

(The king's messenger sets off to find a definition.)

—————. *Tuck Everlasting*. Farrar, 1975.

(Ten-year-old Winnie Foster longs for adventure until she meets the Tuck family and learns the secret of the spring that gave them everlasting life.)

Banks, Lynne Reid. *The Indian in the Cupboard*. Doubleday, 1981.

(English boy's miniature plastic toy Indian comes to life.)

Beatty, Patricia. *Eight Mules from Monterey*. Morrow, 1982.

(Librarian and her daughter take books to California hill settlements in 1916.)

—————. *That's One Ornery Orphan*. Morrow, 1980.

(Hallie May, a homeless girl, looks for a way out of her Texas orphanage.)

Bellairs, John. *The Treasure of Alpheus Winterborn*. Illus. by Judith Gwyn Brown. Harcourt, 1978.

(While working in the town library, thirteen-year-old Anthony finds the first clue to a treasure hidden decades ago by the town's wealthy practical joker.)

Brittain, Bill. *Devil's Donkey*. Illus. by Andrew Glass. Harper, 1981.

(Dan'l Pitt angers a witch and the devil himself after he cuts a branch off the Coven Tree.)

—————. *The Wish Giver: Three Tales of Coven Tree*. Illus. by Andrew Glass. Harper, 1983.

(At the Coven Tree Church Social, three children each spend fifty cents for wish cards that turn their dreams into living nightmares. Sequel to *Devil's Donkey*.)

Burnford, Sheila. *The Incredible Journey*. Illus. by Carl Burger. Little, 1961.

(Two pet dogs and a Siamese cat brave the Canadian wilds on their 250-mile trip home.)

Burnham, Sophy. *Buccaneer*. Illus. by Mike Eagle. Warne, 1977.

(Nothing Julie does pleases her disapproving father, especially when it comes to training an unridable horse.)

Byars, Betsy. *The Summer of the Swans*. Illus. by Ted CoConis. Viking, 1970.

(When Sara's retarded brother disappears, her daylong search helps her begin to understand herself better.)

—————. *The Two-Thousand-Pound Goldfish*. Harper, 1982.

(Warren yearns for his mother, a radical underground fugitive wanted by the FBI, and invents horror movie scenarios as his own escape from life's rougher moments. Hard-hitting intensity mixed with humor; a class discussion of the difference between legitimate protest and extremism should prove worthwhile.)

Callen, Larry. *The Deadly Mandrake.* Illus. by Larry Johnson. Little, 1978.
(Evil lurks in the town of Four Corners after Sorrow Nix's father dies. Sequel to *Pinch.*)

—————. *Pinch.* Illus. by Marvin Friedman. Little, 1975.
(Small town boy trains his new pig in hopes of winning a bird hunting contest.)

—————. *Sorrow's Song.* Illus. by Marvin Friedman. Little, 1979.
(Pinch's mute friend tries to shield a wounded whooping crane from the men who seek it.)

Collier, James Lincoln and Christopher. *My Brother Sam Is Dead.* Four Winds, 1974.
(Revolutionary War conflict within a Tory family when one son joins the Minutemen.)

Conford, Ellen. *And This Is Laura.* Little, 1977.
(Laura considers herself the unexceptional one in her talented family until she discovers her gift of predicting the future.)

—————. *Lenny Kandell, Smart Aleck.* Illus. by Walter Gaffney-Kessell. Little, 1983.
(1940s boy is determined to become a great stand-up comic in spite of the bully who is out to get him.)

Dahl, Roald. *Danny, the Champion of the World.* Illus. by Jill Bennett. Knopf, 1975.
(Boy and his marvelous father go pheasant poaching in Hazell's Wood.)

—————. *The Wonderful Story of Henry Sugar and Six More.* Knopf, 1977.
(Seven mystifying tales, some purportedly autobiographical. Don't miss "The Hitchhiker.")

Du Bois, William Pène. *The Giant.* Viking, 1954.
(While touring Europe to complete work on "A Bear's Guide to the World's Pleasure Spots," the author meets El Muchacho, the biggest boy on Earth.)

—————. *The Twenty-One Balloons.* Viking, 1947.
(An account of Professor Sherman's fantastic balloon voyage to the island of Krakatoa before the volcanic eruption of 1883. A Newbery winner.)

Fife, Dale. *North of Danger.* Illus. by Haakon Saether. Dutton, 1978.

(Norwegian boy must brave snow and hardships to warn his father of the impending Nazi occupation. A thrilling survival story.)

Fisk, Nicholas. *Grinny: A Novel of Science Fiction.* Nelson, 1974.

(Could Great Aunt Emma really be an evil alien from space?)

Fitzhugh, Louise. *Harriet the Spy.* Harper, 1964.

(Girl snooper's secret notebook is filched by her curious and indignant classmates.)

Fleischman, Paul. *The Half-a-Moon Inn.* Illus. by Kathy Jacobi. Harper, 1980.

(While searching for his mother, a mute boy takes shelter at an eerie inn where he is held captive by the ominous old proprietress, Miss Grackle.)

Fleischman, Sid. *The Ghost in the Noonday Sun.* Illus. by Warren Chappell. Little, 1965.

(Oliver is kidnapped by pirates intent on using him to help them find Gentleman Jack's buried treasure.)

—————. *Jingo Django.* Illus. by Eric von Schmidt. Little, 1971.

(Jingo Hawks meets up with gypsies in his search for his scoundrel father.)

George, Jean Craighead. *Julie of the Wolves.* Illus. by John Schoenherr. Harper, 1972.

(Torn between her Eskimo traditions and modern life, Miyax runs away and lives with the wolves on the Alaskan tundra. A Newbery Award winner.)

Grahame, Kenneth. *The Wind in the Willows.* Illus. by Michael Hague. Holt, 1980.

(Classic river tale of Ratty, Mole, Badger, and Toad of Toad Hall.)

Hayes, William. *Project: GENIUS.* Atheneum, 1962.

(Pete's attempts to win first prize for the school science project all backfire. A source of inspiration for your own science curriculum.)

Heath, W.L. *Max the Great.* Illus. by Dorothy Koda. Crane, 1977.

(An organ grinder's monkey attempts to take over a hound dog's popularity in a small Southern town.)

Heide, Florence Parry. *Banana Twist.* Holiday, 1978.

(Jonah D. Krock, TV and fast food freak, meets up with Goober, the world's creepiest neighbor.)

Holland, Isabelle. *Alan and the Animal Kingdom*. Lippincott, 1977.
(Fearful that the authorities will take away his precious animals, Alan keeps the death of his only relative a secret and stays alone in her New York City apartment.)

Hunter, Mollie. *The Wicked One*. Harper, 1977.
(Scottish tale of mischievous supernatural creature who plagues a quick-tempered farmer and his family.)

Hurmence, Belinda. *A Girl Called Boy*. Clarion, 1982.
(Rebellious modern girl finds herself a slave in 1850s North Carolina.)

Juster, Norton. *The Phantom Tollbooth*. Illus. by Jules Feiffer. Random, 1961.
(The ultimate in fantasy, as Milo journeys to Dictionopolis and Digitopolis with Tock, a ticking watchdog. Build your language arts curriculum around this one.)

Kennedy, Richard. *Inside My Feet*. Illus. by Ronald Himler. Harper, 1979.
(Horrifying tale of a boy who saves himself and his parents from a pair of enchanted boots and the giant who controls them.)

King-Smith, Dick. *Pigs Might Fly*. Illus. by Mary Rayner. Viking, 1982.
(Daggie Dogfoot, the runt of the litter, proves himself.)

Korman, Gordon. *This Can't Be Happening at Macdonald Hall*. Illus. by Affie Mohammed. Scholastic, 1978 (pbk. only).
(Headmaster Sturgeon, alias The Fish, tries to split up the infamous roommate team of Boots and Bruno. See also *Beware the Fish* (Scholastic, 1980), the wild sequel.

Lawson, Robert. *Ben and Me*. Little, 1939.
("A New and Astonishing LIFE of BENJAMIN FRANKLIN As written by his Good Mouse AMOS.")

L'Engle, Madeleine. *A Wrinkle in Time*. Farrar, 1962.
(Meg travels with her little brother and friend through time and space to rescue her scientist father from the sinister planet of Camazotz. A Newbery winner.)

McSwigan, Marie. *Snow Treasure*. Illus. by Andre LaBlanc. Dutton, 1942.
(Children in a small Norwegian village save millions of dollars' worth of gold bullion from the clutches of the Nazis during World War II. Based on a true event.)

Merrill, Jean. *The Pushcart War*. Illus. by Ronni Solbert. Addison, 1964.
(Pushcart peddlers battle the giant trucks in New York City.)

Morey, Walt. *Gentle Ben.* Illus. by John Schoenherr. Dutton, 1965.
(Mark struggles to keep his beloved "pet," a wild Alaskan brown bear.)

—————. *Sandy and the Rock Star.* Dutton, 1979.
(Paul, a fifteen-year-old singing idol, runs away to an island where he tries to save a trained cougar from sure death.)

Newman, Robert. *The Case of the Baker Street Irregular.* Atheneum, 1978.
(After being taken to London by his tutor, Anthony must seek aid from the world's greatest detective, Mr. Sherlock Holmes.)

North, Sterling. *Rascal: A Memoir of a Better Era.* Illus. by John Schoenherr. Dutton, 1963.
(A true account of the author's eleventh year, when he caught and raised a wild baby raccoon.)

Norton, Mary. *The Borrowers.* Illus. by Beth and Joe Krush. Harcourt, 1953.
(About the tiny family that lives under the old grandfather clock and makes a living borrowing from "human beans." First in a series.)

O'Brien, Robert C. *Mrs. Frisby and the Rats of NIMH.* Illus. by Zena Bernstein. Atheneum, 1971.
(Brilliant laboratory rats plot their escape from the National Institute of Mental Health. A Newbery winner.)

O'Dell, Scott. *The Black Pearl.* Illus. by Milton Johnson. Houghton, 1967.
(Suspense adventure set in Baja California of Ramon, a teenager who seeks the elusive pearl from the undersea clutches of Manta Diablo.)

—————. *Island of the Blue Dolphins.* Houghton, 1960.
(Early 1800s survival story of an Indian girl who spends eighteen years alone on an island off the California coast. A Newbery winner.)

Paterson, Katherine. *Bridge to Terabithia.* Illus. by Donna Diamond. Crowell, 1977.
(When Leslie moves to Lark Creek, Jess loses his chance to be fastest runner in school, but gains an invaluable friend. A Newbery winner of friendship and devastating loss.)

Pearce, Philippa. *Tom's Midnight Garden.* Illus. by Susan Einzig. Lippincott, 1958.
(During Tom's visit to his aunt and uncle, he goes back in time to meet a girl named Hattie.)

Pfeffer, Susan Beth. *What Do You Do When Your Mouth Won't Open?* Illus. by Lorna Tomei. Delacorte, 1981.
(Reesa sets out to cure her public speaking phobia when she wins an essay contest that requires her to read her composition to a large audience.)

Roberts, Willo Davis. *The Girl with the Silver Eyes.* Atheneum, 1980.
(Although her telekenetic powers have always made her seem different, Katie discovers she is not the only one with unusual abilities.)

—————. *The Minden Curse.* Illus. by Sherry Streeter. Atheneum, 1978.
(Danny's "curse" puts him in the middle of mystery and mayhem when he visits his grandparents at Indian Lake.)

—————. *The View from the Cherry Tree.* Atheneum, 1975.
(Everyone called it a tragic accident, but what Rob witnessed was Old Lady Calloway's murder, and no one will believe him. Fast-paced and suspenseful.)

Robertson, Keith. *Henry Reed's Baby-Sitting Service.* Illus. by Robert McCloskey. Viking, 1966.
(Henry and his friend Midge earn money and trouble with their new summer jobs. One of several in the witty "Henry Reed" series.)

Sargent, Sarah. *Weird Henry Berg.* Crown, 1980.
(Henry's antique egg hatches, yielding a baby dragon. Original and entertaining.)

Sauer, Julia L. *Fog Magic.* Illus. by Lynd Ward. Viking, 1943.
(Greta, who loves the fog, finds she can go through it back in time to a village of her ancestors.)

Shyer, Marlene Fanta. *My Brother, the Thief.* Scribner, 1980.
(Carolyn suspects her half-brother of shoplifting and more.)

—————. *Welcome Home, Jellybean.* Scribner, 1978.
(Neil's thirteen-year-old retarded sister comes home to live.)

Skurzynski, Gloria. *What Happened in Hamelin.* Four Winds, 1979.
(How the Pied Piper led the children away, told by the boy who stayed behind. Based on a true event that took place in Germany during the Middle Ages.)

Sleator, William. *Into the Dream.* Illus. by Ruth Sanderson. Dutton, 1979.

(Two children discover they're both having the same terrifying dream each night.)

Slote, Alfred. *The Devil Rides with Me and Other Fantastic Stories.* Methuen, 1980.
(Sci-fi and other clever short stories.)

Smith, Alison. *Help! There's a Cat Washing in Here.* Illus. by Amy Rowen. Dutton, 1981.
(Henry takes care of the housework while his mother prepares for a new job.)

Speare, Elizabeth George. *The Sign of the Beaver.* Houghton, 1983.
(Alone in his family's cabin in the Maine wilderness of 1768, thirteen-year-old Matt learns about survival from an aloof Indian boy.)

Streatfeild, Noel. *When the Sirens Wailed.* Illus. by Judith Gwyn Brown. Random, 1976.
(The three Clark children are evacuated from London to the countryside during World War II.)

Tannen, Mary. *The Wizard Children of Finn.* Knopf, 1981.
(A wise-cracking girl and her little brother are transported back to ancient Ireland with an enchanted boy. See also the spendid 1982 sequel, *The Lost Legend of Finn.)*

Uchida, Yoshiko. *Journey Home.* Illus. by Charles Robinson. Atheneum, 1978.
(Problems of a Japanese-American family after leaving Topaz, a World War II concentration camp in Utah. Sequel to *Journey to Topaz.* Scribner, 1971).

Ullman, James Ramsey. *Banner in the Sky.* Lippincott, 1954.
(Rudi yearns to conquer the Citadel, a great Swiss mountain where his father, a guide, died fifteen years before.)

Wallace, Barbara Brooks. *Peppermints in the Parlor.* Atheneum, 1980.
(Orphaned little rich girl becomes a servant when she arrives at her aunt's mansion and finds it under the iron rule of the wicked Mrs. Meeching.)

Walsh, Jill. *The Green Book.* Illus. by Lloyd Bloom. Farrar, 1982.
(Thought-provoking account of a family that helps settle a new planet after Earth's demise.)

Wolitzer, Hilma. *Introducing Shirley Braverman.* Farrar, 1975.
(About growing up in Brooklyn during the last year of World War II.)

Wuorio, Eva-Lis. *Code: Polonaise.* Holt, 1971.
(During the Nazi occupation of Poland, a group of brave, homeless children in Warsaw start an underground newspaper.)
York, Carol Beach. *I Will Make You Disappear.* Nelson, 1974.
(After moving into a cheerless summer house, the Astin children discover a witch's room hidden under the shed.)

Illustration from DEVIL'S DONKEY by Bill Brittain. Text copyright © 1981 by William Brittain. Illustrations copyright © 1981 by Andrew Glass. Reproduced by permission of Harper & Row, Publishers, Inc.

Folk and Fairy Tales: Storytelling for Everyone

I used to think that reading aloud to my classes was suffi-cient, that storytelling was too difficult, and that I'd never have the time or talent to learn stories to tell. How experi-ence can change one's thinking! Recently, at a librarian's conference on storytelling, I heard a workshop presenter re-port to her audience, "I'm a school librarian, and so I don't have time to learn stories to tell. Instead, I read to my stu-dents, and now I'll show you how I do that." Shades of my own past, I thought, yet I was shocked at the audacity of another professional to negate the whole purpose of the meeting by instructing her peers in a skill they already know so well. The presenter then read aloud one entire picture book and a chapter from a well-known fiction book to the polite but incredulous spectators who had come, after all, to find out more about the "mysterious" art of storytelling.

The mystery is that teachers and librarians are afraid to tell stories for fear of somehow doing it "wrong." Walk into any teacher's room, and what do you hear? Stories to curl one's hair. Scratch an itchy kid, and what do you get? Eleven corny jokes that have been passed around for the last dec-ade. (Now *there's* the oral tradition in progress.) Anyone can tell a story, and once you've tried it several times, you'll un-derstand what you've been missing and will try it some more. Right ways and wrong ways need not enter into it. Children love stories, but very few have ever heard stories live, with no text, no illustrations, and no commercial breaks for probing questions.

The sharing of folktales, the world's oral and earliest form of communication and literature, which have been handed down from parent to child for generations, should also be a standard part of the classroom reading program. The study of folktales not only enriches any basic social studies curricu-lum, in that it helps children to uncover the universal quali-ties of humankind, but also lays the groundwork for under-standing all literature as well. From kindergarten through the intermediate grades, storytelling can be used as a tool to reinforce comprehension skills, encourage creativity, and stimulate interest in independent reading.

This is the electronic era, when children spend uncounta-ble out-of-school hours watching television or playing video games and in-school time watching films, educational TV and filmstrips, and learning to be computer-ably literate. While the merits of all this plug-in time can be pondered on both sides, teachers can compensate for the affection, emotion, and personal contact that this machinery does not provide. When television tells a story, it offers the viewer no eye contact, no response, and no reason to become emotionally enticed, because the images are preprogrammed, cuing in manufactured laughter and tears at proscribed intervals. Storytelling provides children with drama that speaks to each individual and allows us to let our imaginations flourish.

The first time I was hooked on a story was in the summer of 1980. Professional storyteller Laura Simms was the new instructor at the Rutgers University Graduate School of Library Service, teaching Oral Literature and Traditional Narration—a fancy name for storytelling—and I enrolled in the class. My expectations were not high; aside from Pete Seeger, I had never seen a storyteller close up. As Laura began recounting "Delgadina and the Snake," I was skeptical and determined to stay aloof. Five minutes into the tale, I and all my fellow students one by one were sucked into the narrative. Maybe it was more of a click, or even a swoon, but we all became embedded in the landscape of the story. Amazingly enough, I felt as though Laura were telling that tale to me alone, and I concentrated so hard that I could envision the giant red snake, the wicked witch, her ugly daughter, and the lovely, long-suffering Delgadina. Magic is not reserved for children alone.

Folktales have universal appeal. They are usually short, have fast-moving plots, are often humorous, and almost always end happily. Wishes do come true, but not without the sacrifices of the hero, most often the youngest, weakest child who overcomes the label of dummling, nitwit, or fool. Yes, many of the tales contain violence, but it is violence resolved, with good triumphing over evil, the powerless fighting for deserved recognition, and the tyrannical wrongdoers punished. Folktales instill values without preaching or condescending and provide a way out through fantasy for children who are looking to resolve life's problems. Certainly, these tales would never have lingered so long if they were inconsequential or meaningless.

As teachers and librarians, we often assume that children are familiar with what are, to us, obvious subjects. When I told a third grade class the story of "Rumpelstiltskin," I was appalled to discover that many of the children had never heard it or some of the other basic and well-known tales. Many students in my kindergarten classes had heard only the bowdlerized, Disney-fied version of "Little Red Riding Hood." Whereas I, as a librarian, assumed that children still heard the old, familiar folktales told at home, it seems that this practice is no longer common. If students are not to be deprived of a fundamental form of their literary heritage, perhaps it is incumbent upon us as educators to fill this gap. A study of folklore should be part of every school curriculum, as well as an extension of the classroom basal readers, which usually include a few folktales as one more source of literature.

Learning Stories To Tell

The first step in learning a story is to find one that you love madly. Pick any old tale, and you'll end up hating it before you've ever told it. The story must somehow touch you or tickle you or intrigue you in an unforgettable way.

As I was brushing my teeth one bland morning, reading Yoshiko Uchida's *The Sea of Gold,* a superb collection of Japanese folktales, I was jarred into wakefulness by Cupid's arrow. I fell in love with "The Terrible Black Snake's Revenge," about a timid man named Badger who unwittingly outsmarts the terrible black snake of the mountains. I vowed to learn that story and started working on it that very week.

The search for a tellable tale is often an elusive one. You'll read collections hand-over-fist with no spark, then— WHAM—a folktale will leap out and leave you breathless. Photocopy that story for your files right away, or you will undoubtedly forget where you found it when you are finally all set to learn it. I keep one file of stories already learned and another of stories to be learned. Then, when the urge hits to learn a new story, I go through the file and pick the one that best fits my mood and the occasion.

Storyteller Laura Simms lists five steps to learn a new story: read (or hear it told), outline, discuss, contemplate, and tell. You will notice memorization is not one of the steps. Unless you are learning a literary folktale that requires the precise language, you will not want or need to memorize the bulk of your stories. What you aim for is to internalize each saga so that you can remain somewhat faithful to your source while making that tale come alive in your own imagination. Outlining a story, whether in written or mental form, helps to clarify the sequence. Discussing the plot with an interested friend allows you to flesh out the story and clarify form and details. Contemplating the characters' voices and appearance, the meaning of the story, and your personal approach to telling it will add depth to your performance.

Time is required. Some quick-study types can read a story once and tell it the next day. I like the tape recorder approach to storytelling. I can read my selection twenty-seven times and still forget who flummoxes whom, but once I've taped myself reading the original story, I listen to it for a week or so while driving to work, tell it aloud on the expressway every morning, and PRESTO, I'm ready for a real audience. Whatever method you use, practice telling the tale out loud until it sounds smooth and you feel at ease.

Storytelling should be an engrossing experience for your audience, so strut your stuff in front of a mirror, your spouse, the cat, or even the portulaca before you go for a crowd. That spontaneous style takes a bit of rehearsal until you are at home with your story. At that point, allow no delay—TELL THAT TALE. The first time is shaky, the second is better, the third is satisfying, and by the fourth, you'll feel as comfortable as a broken-in loafer.

When you forget a major section, as we all do sometimes, backtrack with the old line, "Now I may not have mentioned it, but. . . ." Weave your mistakes right into the narrative so that they sound like part of the story. If you stop and admit to your listeners that you have left out that essential bit, you lose credibility and break the spell. Think fast and you can save any story.

Start by learning short folktales so that you won't become discouraged and overwhelmed. Kindergarten through second grades are ideal for telling brief, funny, cumulative, or repetitious tales, for children can remember the story's sequence and join in as tellers. In the upper elementary grades, stories should reflect the variety of world cultures, styles, and genres such as myths, legends, fairy tales, and fables. Listen to the range of recorded storytellers, and you will find that each one has developed a unique style. You must tell stories in a way that suits you—whether with or without gestures, using one voice or changing it to fit each character, involving students vocally or not, with props or with none. Never fear—once you start, it's easier than it looks.

Kids Tell Stories

Storytelling adds a refreshing slant to the teaching of comprehension skills. In a project that I developed and conducted with fourth grade classes, the children spent ten weeks learning to become storytellers. My general goals in the "Kids Tell Stories" project were as follows:

1. To familiarize students and teachers with the background and traditions of oral literature,
2. to introduce children to a body of written literature (i.e., folktales),
3. to acquaint students with skills of storytelling and oral expression,
4. to develop the ability of students to conceptualize, using the "mind's eye" to visualize a complete story, and
5. to develop reading and writing skills as an outgrowth of storytelling.

During our sessions we explored the origins of storytelling, read stories from all over the world, charted the types and themes of stories, and discovered the characteristics of main characters. Students dramatized and diagrammed the stories I told, outlined the plots, drew portraits of characters, and constructed maps of the settings. Even after a week, a class, sitting in a circle, could retell an entire story round robin, almost line for line. When one child forgot a section, someone else was sure to recall it.

We read variants of well-known stories, such as a Perrault versus a Grimm version of "Cinderella," Kha's *In the Land of Small Dragon* from Vietnam, and "Cenerentola" from Virginia Haviland's *Favorite Fairy Tales Told in Italy.*

Students performed exercises to hone their storytelling skills by using their voices and bodies to fit the tone and point of view of each character and by learning to breathe properly and to project. They made charts comparing folktale characters, beginnings and endings, and common tale motifs. Finally, each child learned a story to tell, and the class listened to and evaluated each telling.

Each week the classroom teacher supplemented my lesson

by reading aloud a sampling of folktales and by helping students to select and learn their stories. Using the stories as a kickoff to writing was encouraged. For instance, after hearing "Why Dogs Hate Cats" from Julius Lester's *The Knee-High Man*, students made up new stories to explain the ongoing rivalry between mutt and feline.

Since a storyteller is not fulfilled until an audience is enthralled, a goal of the ten weeks was for each "trainee" to tell his or her story to other classes. We used kindergarten, first, and second graders as our willing guinea pigs. The program's success can be measured in part by the number of students who still remembered their stories the following year.

Folktales are familiar allies to most students at Van Holten School, and 398.2, the Dewey number representing fairy tales in the non-fiction section of the library, has become a well-known number to my students. When you walk into the library and look up, you'll see that number prominently displayed on the fairy tale ceiling mural created by one third grade class. And every child has sung the 398.2 song that I wrote to help them remember the number and its significance:

Look for 398.2

If you want a good story, let me tell you what to do,
Look for 398.2.

If dragons are your fancy, shiny tails of green and blue,
Look for 398.2.

Prince or princess in hot water, trouble with a witch's brew,
Look for 398.2.

Ogres, leprechauns and goblins all are waiting there for you,
Look for 398.2.

Find a tale from every country, from Morocco to Peru,
Look for 398.2.

In 1942, famed storyteller Ruth Sawyer wrote in her book *The Way of the Storyteller* (p. 167), "Insecurity, disturbance, apathy, national distrust are everywhere today. If we can make the art of storytelling an applied art, by which we may bring the rich heritage of good books into the lives of children throughout our country, that they may find a universal eagerness toward life and an abiding trust, then I think we may truly help build for the future."

Children never tire of the magical story that makes them laugh or lets them linger in an enchanted world. By giving them the chance to hear stories told and to become storytellers themselves, we are indeed providing for the next generation, continuing an age-old tradition that must not become a victim of progress.

Self-Shining Shoes

Professor Lucifer Gorgonzola Butts A.K. invents simple self-shining shoes- as passerby steps rudely on your shoes, you bend over, causing string (A) to pull open accordion (B), sounding note (C) - dancing mouse (D) starts waltzing and steps on trigger of pistol (E) - bullet (F) disengages hook (G) and allows arrow (H) to shoot out, pulling cord (I) which opens inverted box (J), dropping bone (K) - pet dog (L) sees bone, wags tail, causing brush (M) to spread polish (N) which drops from hole in derby (O).

Folk & Fairy Tales, Myths & Legends

Single Stories

Aardema, Verna. *Bringing the Rain to Kapiti Plain.* Illus. by Beatriz Vidal. Dial, 1981.
(African cumulative tale. Children can join in on each refrain.)

――――――. *The Riddle of the Drum.* Illus. by Tony Chen. Four Winds, 1979.
(Cumulative Mexican folktale of princess' suitor who must prove himself worthy. Listeners will love repeating the name-filled refrain.)

――――――. *What's So Funny, Ketu?* Illus. by Marc Brown. Dial, 1982.
(Mirthful African story of a man who helps a snake and is rewarded with the magic gift of understanding animal speech.)

――――――. *Who's in Rabbit's House?* Illus. by Leo and Diane Dillon. Dial, 1977.
(Masai story of how Rabbit and his friends get The Long One out of the house. Perfect to act out, especially since the illustrations present the story as a play and the characters as costumed actors.)

――――――. *Why Mosquitos Buzz in People's Ears.* Illus. by Leo and Diane Dillon. Dial, 1975.
(Cumulative African folktale. Fun for recalling sequence and acting out.)

Aliki. *The Twelve Months.* Greenwillow, 1978.
(Greek folktale of a poor, humble widow and a jealous, rich one who each get what they deserve. Compare with De Regniers's *Little Sister and the Month Brothers* and Marshak's *The Month Brothers.*)

Andersen, Hans Christian. *The Princess and the Pea.* Illus. by Paul Galdone. Seabury, 1978.
(Even twenty mattresses can't lie in the way of a true princess.)

――――――. *Thumbelina.* Illus. by Adrienne Adams. Scribner, 1961.
(Travels of a tiny girl.)

――――――. *The Ugly Duckling.* Illus. by Adrienne Adams. Scribner, 1965.
(Classic story of a swan's miserable childhood.)

――――――. *The Ugly Duckling.* Illus. by Lorinda Bryan

Cauley. Harcourt, 1979.
(Another beautifully illustrated version.)

Aruego, Jose and Ariane. *A Crocodile's Tale*. Scribner, 1972.
(Phillipine folk story of an ungrateful crocodile who decides to eat Juan after the boy has freed him from a trap. Good to act out with improvised dialogue.)

Asbjørnsen, P.C. *The Runaway Pancake*. Illus. by Svend Otto S. Larousse, 1980.
(Funny Norwegian cumulative tale. Fine to act out and to compare with variants such as Galdone's *The Gingerbread Boy* and Sawyer's *Journey Cake, Ho!*)

————. *The Squire's Bride*. Illus. by Marcia Sewell. Atheneum, 1975.
(The Squire wants to marry the farmer's pretty young daughter, but she is not interested in the least.)

————. *The Three Billy Goats Gruff*. Illus. by Marcia Brown. Harcourt, 1957.
(Classic Norwegian tale of a nasty troll who gets his. Perfect to dramatize using improvised dialogue. Compare with the version illustrated by Paul Galdone.)

Baker, Olaf. *Where the Buffaloes Begin*. Illus. by Stephen Gammell. Warne, 1981.
(American Indian story of Little Wolf who finds the fabled buffalo lake and saves his people from a marauding tribe. For grades 3–6.)

Bang, Molly Garrett. *Tye May and the Magic Brush*. Greenwillow, 1981.
(A poor Chinese girl's paintings come to life, much to the envy of the greedy emperor.)

————. *Wiley and the Hairy Man*. Macmillan, 1976.
(Black American folktale about a boy who must fool the swamp-dwelling Hairy Man three times to be rid of him.)

Barth, Edna. *Jack-O'-Lantern*. Illus. by Paul Galdone. Seabury, 1974.
(American Halloween fare of how ornery Jack outwitted the Devil. Best appreciated by grades 3–6.)

Basile, Giambattista. *Petrosinella: A Neopolitan Rapunzel*. Illus. by Diane Stanley. Warne, 1981.
(Compare this elegant Italian variant to the two Grimm renditions illustrated by Trina Schart Hyman and Bernadette Watts. Grades 4–6.)

Belpre, Pura. *Oté*. Illus. by Paul Galdone. Pantheon, 1969.
(Puerto Rican devil and the little boy who foils him. Good play material.)

Blegvad, Erik. *The Three Little Pigs*. Atheneum, 1980.
(You'll be surprised by the number of children who have never heard the whole story. Also check the versions illustrated by Lorinda Bryan Cauley and Paul Galdone.)

Bowden, Joan Chase. *The Bean Boy*. Illus. by Sal Murdocca. Macmillan, 1979.
(Amusing sequence story much like "The Travels of a Fox" which is found in Anne Rockwell's *The Old Woman and Her Pig and Ten Other Stories*, and many other folktale collections. Both stories are satisfying for telling and acting out with improvised dialogue.)

──────. *Why the Tides Ebb and Flow*. Illus. by Marc Brown. Houghton, 1979.
(An original explanation. Use with your science lesson, for all ages.)

Brenner, Barbara. *Little One Inch*. Illus. by Fred Brenner. Coward, 1977.
(Japanese Tom Thumb, named Issun Boshi, meets up with demons in the great outside world.)

Brown, Marcia. *Dick Whittington and His Cat*. Scribner, 1950.
(Classic English story of the poor boy whose cat brought him riches and fame.)

──────. *Stone Soup*. Scribner, 1947.
(French cooking lesson. Use with Harve Zemach's *Nail Soup* and try out the recipes for lunch. A large cast of characters makes it suitable for acting out using improvised dialogue.)

Cauley, Lorinda Bryan. *The Cock, the Mouse and the Little Red Hen*. Putnam, 1982.
(Industrious hen saves them all from a hungry fox.)

──────. *Goldilocks and the Three Bears*. Putnam, 1981.
(Marvelous illustrations give new vitality to this old chestnut. See also Galdone's version, *The Three Bears*.)

──────. *The Goose and the Golden Coins*. Harcourt, 1981.
(Italian folktale about two poor sisters who buy an extraordinary goose.)

──────. *The Three Little Pigs*. Putnam, 1980.
(Humorously and colorfully illustrated. See also versions by Erik Blegvad and Paul Galdone.)

Cheng, Hou-Tien. *The Six Chinese Brothers*. Holt, 1979.
(Scissors cuttings depict the saga of the identical brothers who can not be executed.)

Christan, Mary Blount. *April Fool*. Illus. by Diane Dawson. Macmillan, 1981.
(Foolish behavior by the townsfolk of Gotham convinces King John to build his hunting lodge elsewhere.)

Conger, Lesley. *Tops and Bottoms*. Illus. by Imero Gobbato. Four Winds, 1970.
(How the Devil is outsmarted by a quick-thinking farmer.)

D'Aulaire, Ingri and Edgar Parin. *D'Aulaire's Trolls*. Doubleday, 1972.
(The truth about Norwegian trolls and their relatives, from hulder-maidens to gnomes.)

Dayrell, Elphinstone. *Why the Sun and the Moon Live in the Sky*. Illus. by Blair Lent. Houghton, 1968.
(African folktale explanation that will relate to your astronomy lesson. Children can compose their own explanations.)

De Paola, Tomie, illus. *The Cat on the Dovrefell*. Trans. by Sir George Webbe Dasent. Putnam, 1979.
(Norwegian Christmas yarn about Halvor who, with the help of a large white bear, scares away marauding trolls.)

—————. *Fin M'Coul, the Giant of Knockmany Hill*. Holiday, 1981.
(Irish giant and his clever wife put an end to giant Cucullin's powers.)

—————. *Strega Nona*. Prentice, 1975.
(Italian tale of lotsa pasta. Don't miss the Weston Woods filmstrip version.)

De Regniers, Beatrice Schenk. *Little Sister and the Month Brothers*. Illus. by Margot Tomes. Seabury, 1976.
(Slavic story about a hard-working young girl and the downfall of her malicious stepmother and stepsister. Use with Aliki's *The Twelve Months*, a Greek variant, and Marshak's *The Month Brothers*.)

Domanska, Janina. *King Krakus and the Dragon*. Greenwillow, 1979.
(Ravenous dragon goes on a rampage in the Polish town of Krakow.)

—————. *The Turnip*. Macmillan, 1969.
(Everyone tries to pull it up in this Russian tale, perfect for narrative pantomime. Compare with Alexei Tolstoi's *The Great Big Enormous Turnip*.)

Duff, Maggie. *Rum Pum Pum*. Illus. by Jose Aruego and Ariane Dewey. Macmillan, 1978.
(General Blackbird makes war on the king who has stolen

his wife. A cumulative Indian tale with a lively chant for children to repeat. Practice rolling your "r's".)

Gackenbach, Dick. *Arabella and Mr. Crack*. Macmillan, 1982.
(Short English tale of a new housekeeper who must adapt to her master's eccentric vocabulary. Compare with Marcia Sewall's version of *Master of All Masters*.)

Galdone, Joanna. *The Little Girl and the Big Bear*. Illus. by Paul Galdone. Houghton, 1980.
(After being captured as a bear's servant, Little Girl devises a plan for her escape. A Slavic tale.)

—————. *The Tailypo: A Ghost Story*. Illus. by Paul Galdone. Seabury, 1977.
(Old man is terrified when the varmint whose tail he has chopped off and eaten returns to get him.)

Galdone, Paul. *The Amazing Pig*. Houghton, 1981.
(Hungarian tale teller outwits king by telling him something unbelievable. Afterward, students can hone their own exaggerating skills. Best for grades 2 and up.)

—————. *Cinderella*. McGraw, 1978.
(Classic French fairy tale. Use with numerous variants by Perrault and Grimm, Kha's *In the Land of Small Dragon*, and Louie's *Yeh Shen*.)

—————. *The Gingerbread Boy*. Seabury, 1975.
(Cookie escapes only to meet his end in the jaws of a fox. Chant the refrain together and/or act out. Also see Sawyer's *Journey Cake, Ho!*)

—————. *Henny Penny*. Seabury, 1968.
("The sky is falling!" cries the simple hen when struck on the head by a falling acorn.)

—————. *King of the Cats*. Houghton, 1980.
(A gravedigger witnesses cats' midnight funeral. Listeners will be eager to supply sound effects. Grades 2–6.)

—————. *The Little Red Hen*. Seabury, 1973.
(Lazy cat, dog, and mouse refuse to help out with the bread-making chores. Children can chime in on the "Not I" refrain.)

—————. *The Magic Porridge Pot*. Seabury, 1976.
(It overflows. Fun to use with Tomie de Paola's *Strega Nona*.)

—————. *The Monkey and the Crocodile*. Seabury, 1969.
(Fable from India of a hungry croc and the cunning monkey he plans to eat.)

—————. *The Monster and the Tailor*. Clarion, 1982.

(While stitching the Grand Duke's trousers in the grave-yard, the tailor must fend off a horrific monster.)

——————. *The Old Woman and Her Pig*. McGraw, 1960. (Cumulative English folktale of the dog, stick, fire, water, ox, butcher, rat, and cat needed to nudge a stubborn pig. Plenty of parts for acting out in narrative pantomime.)

——————. *The Three Bears*. Seabury, 1972. (Goldilocks strikes again. Also check out Lorinda Bryan Cauley's version.)

——————. *The Three Billy Goats Gruff*. Seabury, 1973. ("Who's that tripping over my bridge?" Compare with another version of the P.C. Asbjornsen story illustrated by Marcia Brown.)

——————. *The Three Little Pigs*. Seabury, 1970. (See also versions by Lorinda Bryan Cauley and Erik Bleg-vad.)

——————. *The Three Sillies*. Clarion, 1981. (English noodlehead tale of a suitor who sets out to find three people who are sillier than his sweetheart and her parents.)

——————. *The Three Wishes*. McGraw, 1961. (English woodsman wastes his fairy-given wishes when he craves a link of black pudding.)

——————. *What's in Fox's Sack?* Clarion, 1982. (Greedy fox parlays his fortune from bee to boy. A good tale to act out; check Anne Rockwell's *The Old Woman and Her Pig and Ten Other Stories* for another version.)

Ginsburg, Mirra. *The Magic Stove*. Illus. by Linda Heller. Coward, 1983. (Russian king steals a poor couple's little stove that makes pies on command.)

——————. *The Night It Rained Pancakes*. Illus. by Douglas Florian. Greenwillow, 1980. (Humorous Russian tale of two peasant brothers who find a way to keep the pot of gold they dug up.)

Grimm, Jacob. *The Bearskinner*. Illus. by Felix Hoffman. Atheneum, 1978. (Young soldier's deal with the Devil includes wearing a bearskin as a cloak and not bathing for seven years. Grades 2–4.)

——————. *Cinderella*. Illus. by Nonny Hogrogian. Green-willow, 1981. (In this telling, Cinderella is aided by white doves and a hazel tree. Compare with the Perrault or Paul Galdone versions as well as Asian variants, *In the Land of Small Dragon* by Kha and *Yeh-Shen* by Louie.)

—————. *The Devil with the Three Golden Hairs.* Illus. by Nonny Hogrogian. Knopf, 1983.
(King is determined to thwart the poor boy who is destined to marry the princess.)

—————. *The Fisherman and His Wife.* Trans. by Elizabeth Shub. Illus. by Monika Laimgruber. Greenwillow, 1978.
(Not satisfied with the wish granted by a magic fish, a covetous woman demands more. Compare with the Margot Zemach version below. Grades 2–4.)

—————. *The Fisherman and His Wife.* Trans. by Randall Jarrell. Illus. by Margot Zemach. Farrar, 1980.
(Riotous illustrations mark this version; compare with the glowing paintings in the Monika Laimgruber edition above. Grades 2–4.)

—————. *The Frog Prince.* Illus. by Paul Galdone. McGraw, 1974.
(After the frog retrieves the princess' golden ball from the bottom of the well, he visits the palace to make her keep her promise.)

—————. *Hans in Luck.* Illus. by Paul Galdone. Parents, 1979.
(Hans takes his wages for seven years' work and makes trade after trade, ending up with nothing. Similar in theme to Wiesner's *Happy-Go-Lucky.*)

—————. *Hansel and Gretel.* Trans. by Charles Scribner, Jr. Illus. by Adrienne Adams. Scribner, 1975.
(Two children find their way to a witch's gingerbread house after being abandoned in the woods by their parents. Compare with the Galdone illustrated version below.)

—————. *Hansel and Gretel.* Illus. by Paul Galdone. McGraw, 1982.
(More proof that wicked witches do not prevail. Also see the Adrienne Adams version above.)

—————. *Jorinda and Joringel.* Trans. by Elizabeth Shub. Illus. by Adrienne Adams. Scribner, 1968.
(A witch who turns maidens into caged birds puts her spell on two young sweethearts.)

—————. *Little Brother and Little Sister.* Illus. by Barbara Cooney. Doubleday, 1982.
(After fleeing their wicked stepmother, Little Brother is transformed into a faun.)

—————. *Little Red Cap*. Illus. by Lisbeth Zwerger. Morrow, 1983.
(Delicately illustrated version of a universally known tale. Compare with Grimm's *Little Red Riding Hood* listed below, illustrated by Paul Galdone and Trina Schart Hyman, and with Harper's *The Gunniwolf*.)

—————. *Little Red Riding Hood*. Illus. by Paul Galdone. McGraw, 1974.
(Many children have never heard the traditional version of the wolf in Granny's clothing. Compare with the other editions by Trina Schart Hyman and Lisbeth Zwerger's *Little Red Cap* and Wilhelmina Harper's *The Gunni Wolf*.)

—————. *Little Red Riding Hood*. Illus. by Trina Schart Hyman. Holiday, 1983.
(Another splendid rendition. Compare with other Grimm retellings illustrated by Paul Galdone and Lisbeth Zwerger and with Harper's *The Gunni Wolf*.

—————. *Rapunzel*. Retold by Barbara Rogasky. Illus. by Trina Schart Hyman. Holiday, 1982.
(Handsomely illustrated retelling of the story of a young maid locked in a tower with only her opulent tresses for company. See also the edition illustrated by Bernadette Watts and the Italian variant, *Petrosinella,* retold by Giambattista Basile.)

—————. *Rapunzel*. Illus. by Bernadette Watts. Crowell, 1975.
(A colorful, primitive style marks the paintings in this retelling. Compare both this and the above book illustrated by Trina Schart Hyman with the Italian variant *Petrosinella* by Giambattista Basile.)

—————. *Rumpelstiltskin*. Illus. by Jacqueline Ayer. Harcourt, 1967.
(As a reward for spinning straw into gold, the little man demands the miller's daughter's first-born child. See also the version retold by Tarcov, Ness's *Tom Tit Tot,* and Zemach's *Duffy and the Devil*.)

—————. *Rumpelstiltskin*. Retold by Edith Tarcov. Illus. by Edward Gorey. Four Winds, 1973.
(Miller's daughter must guess his name or forfeit her child. Compare to version above, illustrated by Ayer, and to Ness's *Tom Tit Tot,* and Zemach's *Duffy and the Devil*.)

—————. *The Shoemaker and the Elves*. Illus. by Adrienne Adams. Scribner, 1961.
(The luck of a poor cobbler changes when the wee men pay him several visits. A fine candidate for improvised drama.)

—————. *The Sleeping Beauty*. Illus. by Trina Schart Hyman. Little, 1977.
(The prophecy of a wicked fairy comes true when Briar Rose pricks her finger and falls into a hundred-year sleep. See also Grimm's *Thorn Rose*. Grades 2–5.)

—————. *Snow White*. Trans. by Paul Heins. Illus. by Trina Schart Hyman. Little, 1974.
(A gloomy forest and seven dwarfs await the lovely young girl who has aroused her stepmother's murderous jealousy. Grades 2–5.)

—————. *The Table, the Donkey and the Stick*. Illus. by Paul Galdone. McGraw, 1976.
(Thanks to a lying goat, three brothers are sent into the world to seek their fortunes.)

—————. *Thorn Rose or, The Sleeping Beauty*. Illus. by Errol LeCain. Bradbury, 1977.
(Another gloriously illustrated edition of the tale of a princess' hundred-year snooze. See also Grimm's *The Sleeping Beauty*, illustrated by Trina Schart Hyman.)

—————. *The Twelve Dancing Princesses*. Illus. by Errol LeCain. Viking, 1978.
(With the aid of a cloak that makes him invisible, a sharp-witted soldier solves the mystery of their nightly disappearances.)

—————. *The Valiant Little Tailor*. Illus. by Victor Ambrus. Oxford, 1980.
(After the tailor kills seven flies with one blow, he takes on two giants. See Christine Price's *Sixty at a Blow* for a similar story from Turkey.)

Hague, Kathleen and Michael. *East of the Sun and West of the Moon*. Illus. by Michael Hague. Harcourt, 1980.
(Norwegian girl seeks her love after ignoring his advice and discovering his identity. Grades 3–5.)

—————. *The Man Who Kept House*. Illus. by Michael Hague. Harcourt, 1981.
(Norwegian story of a housewife and her farmer husband who swap jobs for one day. See also Wiesner's *Turnabout*.)

Haley, Gail E. *A Story, A Story*. Atheneum, 1970.
(African tale of Anansi the Spider and how he spread the world's first stories. A Caldecott winner.)

Hardendorff, Jeanne. *The Bed Just So*. Illus. by Lisl Weil. Four Winds, 1975.
(Tailor tries to find a suitable bed for the unseen hudgin that lives in the house. Children can repeat each refrain.)

Harper, Wilhelmina. *The Gunniwolf.* Illus. by William Wiesner. Dutton, 1946.

(Little Girl breaks her promise to her mother when she wanders into the jungle and meets up with the Gunniwolf. Compare this variant with any of the Grimm versions of *Little Red Riding Hood* listed above. Act out in pairs.)

Harris, Rosemary. *Beauty and the Beast.* Illus. by Errol LeCain. Doubleday, 1980.

(To save her father's life, the merchant's youngest daughter agrees to move to the palace of a monstrous beast. Compare with Marianna Mayer's retelling. Grades 2–5.)

Hawthorne, Nathaniel. *The Golden Touch.* Illus. by Paul Galdone. McGraw, 1959.

(King Midas learns his lesson after he turns his own daughter into gold.)

Hirsch, Marilyn. *Could Anything Be Worse?* Holiday, 1974.

(Yiddish folktale of a frustrated man and his overcrowded house. Has a large cast for acting out with improvised dialogue. Also compare to a similar retelling by Margot Zemach entitled *It Could Always Be Worse.*)

—————. *The Rabbi and the Twenty-Nine Witches.* Holiday, 1976.

(Based on a Talmudic tale of a rabbi who finds a way for the villagers to see the full moon.)

Hodges, Margaret. *The Little Humpbacked Horse.* Illus. by Chris Conover. Farrar, 1980.

(Russian fool prospers with the aid of his wise and faithful horse companion.)

—————. *The Wave.* Illus. by Blair Lent. Houghton, 1964.

(Burning his rice fields is the only way a wealthy old Japanese grandfather can warn the villagers of an impending tidal wave.)

Hogrogian, Nonny. *One Fine Day.* Macmillan, 1971.

(Caldecott Medal cumulative tale of a fox who must barter for milk to give to an old woman before she will sew his tail back on. Children can retell in sequence and act out.)

Hurlimann, Ruth. *The Proud White Cat.* Trans. by Anthea Bell. Morrow, 1977.

(In this German sequence story, Tom Cat asks Mrs. Vixen the fox for advice about the worthiest lady for him to marry.)

Hutton, Warwick. *The Nose Tree.* Atheneum, 1980.

(Apples from a nose-growing tree enable three soldiers to retrieve their magical possessions from a scheming princess. See also Zemach's earthy version, *Too Much Nose.*)

Jameson, Cynthia. *One for the Price of Two*. Illus. by Anita Lobel. Parents, 1972.
(An old Japanese man is cured of bragging after his fine new heifer disappears.)

Keats, Ezra Jack. *John Henry: An American Legend*. Pantheon, 1965.
(How the steel-driving man beat the steam drill and died with his hammer in his hand.)

Kha, Dang Manh. *In the Land of Small Dragon: A Vietnamese Folktale*. Illus. by Tony Chen. Viking, 1979.
(Magnificent Cinderella variant. Contrast with other retellings such as Louie's *Yen-Shen* and Grimm's and Perrault's *Cinderella*.)

Louie, Ai-Ling. *Yeh-Shen: A Cinderella Story from China*. Philomel, 1982.
(A magic fish is the girl's confidant in this tale that predates by one thousand years the earliest known European version. Compare with stories by Grimm, Perrault, Galdone, and Kha's *In the Land of Small Dragon*.)

Maitland, Antony. *Idle Jack*. Farrar, 1979.
(Lazy English noodlehead tries to earn an honest living.)

Marshak, Samuel. *The Month Brothers: A Slavic Tale*. Trans. by Thomas P. Whitney. Illus. by Diane Stanley.
(Czechoslovakian story about a girl sent by her stepmother into a winter blizzard to pick snowdrops. Compare with Beatrice Schenk de Regniers's *Little Sister and the Month Brothers* and Aliki's *The Twelve Months*. Marshak produced the play in postwar Russia; you might do the same with your own student actors.)

Mayer, Marianna. *Beauty and the Beast*. Illus. by Mercer Mayer. Four Winds, 1978.
(Compare the lyric text and the voluptuous illustrations with the mannered tapestry style of the Harris version, with pictures by Errol LeCain. Grades 2–5.)

McDermott, Gerald. *Anansi the Spider: A Tale from the Ashanti*. Holt, 1972.
(West African story from Ghana of how the moon came to be.)

—————. *The Voyage of Osiris: A Myth of Ancient Egypt*. Dutton, 1977.
(Dazzling illustrations uplift this account of how Osiris became Lord of the Underworld.)

Mosel, Arlene. *The Funny Little Woman*. Illus. by Blair Lent. Dutton, 1972.

(Japanese ogres kidnap her to become their cook. A Caldecott winner. Look for the superb Weston Woods filmstrip.)

——————. *Tikki Tikki Tembo.* Illus. by Blair Lent. Holt, 1968.

(Chinese tale of a long-named boy who falls into a well. Your children will not be able to resist chanting that great long name every time you do.)

Ness, Evaline. *Mr. Miacca: An English Folktale.* Holt, 1967.

(Bad Tommy Grimes is captured by wicked Mr. Miacca, who plans to boil the boy and eat him for supper.)

——————. *Tom Tit Tot.* Scribner, 1965.

(English variant of "Rumpelstiltskin," told in catchy dialect. Compare with the Grimm versions and Zemach's *Duffy and the Devil.*)

Newton, Patricia Montgomery. *The Five Sparrows: A Japanese Folktale.* Atheneum, 1982.

(After nursing a wounded sparrow, an old woman is rewarded for her kindness.)

Otsuka, Zuzo. *Suho and the White Horse.* Viking, 1981.

(Mongolian legend of a boy and his loyal horse.)

Perrault, Charles. *Cinderella; Or, The Little Glass Slipper.* Illus. by Marcia Brown. Scribner, 1954.

(A Caldecott winner, illustrated in French baroque style. Compare with many versions, including those by Grimm, Galdone, Kha's *In the Land of Small Dragon,* and Louie's *Yeh-Shen.*)

Price, Christine. *Sixty at a Blow: A Tall Tale from Turkey.* Dutton, 1968.

(Kara Mustapha kills sixty flies with his rusty knife and then must vanquish forty giants. Variants of this tale include Grimm's *The Valiant Little Tailor* and Van Woerkom's *Alexandra the Rock-Eater.*)

Proddow, Penelope. *Demeter and Persephone.* Illus. by Barbara Cooney. Doubleday 1972.

(Homeric hymn of the goddess' daughter who is stolen away by Hades, Lord of the Underworld. Read during cold weather as an explanation of winter, and afterward, share a pomegranate with your listeners. Grades 3–6.)

Quigley, Lillian F. *The Blind Men and the Elephant.* Illus. by Janice Holland. Scribner, 1959.

(Indian fable of six blind men who each determine what the great beast is like.)

Ransome, Arthur. *The Fool of the World and the Flying Ship.*

Illus. by Uri Shulevitz. Farrar, 1968.

(Russian Fool wins the Czar's daughter thanks to the singular talents of his travelling companions. A Caldecott winner. Grades 2–4.)

Riordan, James. *The Three Magic Gifts*. Illus. by Errol LeCain. Oxford, 1980.

(Poor Russian man loses his magic cloth and goat to his rich brother. A familiar theme in folklore; compare with Grimm's *The Table, the Donkey and the Stick*.)

Sawyer, Ruth. *Journey Cake, Ho!* Illus. by Robert McCloskey. Viking, 1953.

(Johnny's pancake gets away from him. This American version of a familiar theme includes two refrains for your listeners to sing or chant. Compare to Galdone's *The Gingerbread Boy*.)

Say, Allen. *Once Under the Cherry Blossom Tree: An Old Japanese Tale*. Harper, 1974.

(A miserly village landlord grows a cherry tree on top of his head.)

Scribner, Charles. *The Devil's Bridge*. Illus. by Evaline Ness. Scribner, 1978.

(When a French village's bridge is destroyed in a storm, a sinister stranger appears and offers to rebuild it—for a price. Grades 2–4.)

Severo, Emoke de Papp. *The Good-Hearted Youngest Brother*. Illus. by Diane Goode. Bradbury, 1981.

(A bearded little man assists three Hungarian brothers in breaking the enchantments that transformed three princesses.)

Sewell, Marcia. *Master of All Masters: An English Folktale*. Little, 1972.

(A young servant girl must learn silly new names for ordinary household objects. Compare with the Gackenbach rendition, *Arabella and Mr. Crack*.)

Shulevitz, Uri. *The Magician*. Macmillan, 1973.

(Passover story adapted from a Yiddish tale by I.L. Peretz.)

Small, Ernest. *Baba Yaga*. Illus. by Blair Lent. Houghton, 1966.

(Iron-toothed Russian witch who lives in a hut that walks on chicken legs catches a bad Russian child for her stewpot.)

Spray, Carole. *The Mare's Egg*. Illus. by Kim La Fave. Camden House, 1981.

(Gullible rube settler spends ten dollars for a pumpkin that he thinks will hatch a colt. Similar to *The Gollywhopper*

Egg by Anne Rockwell.)

Stadler, Valerie. *Even the Devil Is Afraid of a Shrew.* Illus. by Richard Brown. Addison, 1972.
(Overwhelmed by his wife's incessant nagging, Pava Jalvi pushes her into a hole where a devil dwells. A boldly illustrated gem from Lapland.)

Stern, Simon. *The Hobyas.* Prentice, 1977.
(Gleeful adaption of Jacob's English tale about the little dog who scares the creatures away from his owners' turnip house. Makes a fine puppet show or a play using repetitive dialogue.)

Still, James. *Jack and the Wonder Beans.* Illus. by Margot Tomes. Putnam, 1977.
(Kentucky-bred "Jack and the Beanstalk," replete with irresistible Appalachian dialect.)

Tolstoi, Alexei. *The Great Big Enormous Turnip.* Illus. by Helen Oxenbury. Heinemann, 1968.
(Everyone must work together to pull it up. Compare with Domanska's *The Turnip* and have your students act it out.)

Tresselt, Alvin. *The Mitten: An Old Ukranian Folktale.* Illus. by Yaroslava. Lothrop, 1964.
(One by one, the forest animals crowd into a boy's lost mitten in order to keep warm.)

Turska, Krystyna. *The Magician of Cracow.* Greenwillow, 1975.
(Polish magician makes a pact with the Devil.)

Van Woerkom, Dorothy. *Alexandra, the Rock-Eater.* Illus. by Rosenkrans Hoffman. Knopf, 1978.
(Russian tale of dragons outwitted by a mother of one hundred children. Compare with Price's *Sixty at a Blow* and Grimm's *The Valiant Little Tailor* for similar exploits.)

Walker, Barbara. *Teeny-Tiny and the Witch Woman.* Illus. by Michael Foreman. Pantheon, 1975.
(Frightening Turkish tale of how the smallest of three brothers saves them all. A variant of Grimm's *Hansel and Gretel.*)

Wiesner, William. *Happy-Go-Lucky.* Seabury, 1970.
(A Norwegian farmer wins a bet after he relates to his wife his misfortunes in selling their cow.)

——————. *Turnabout.* Seabury, 1972.
(A Norwegian farmer, scornful of his wife's housekeeping chores, offers to exchange jobs for the day. See also Hague's *The Man Who Kept House.*)

Wildsmith, Brian. *The Hare and the Tortoise.* Watts, 1966.

(Slow and steady wins every time in this adaptation of seventeenth-century French author La Fontaine's adaptation of an Aesop fable.)

—————. *The Lion and the Rat.* Watts, 1963.

(Mouse repays lion in kind after the lion frees him. A fable by French storyteller La Fontaine, based on the ancient Aesop fable.)

Wolkstein, Diane. *The Banza.* Illus. by Marc Brown. Dial, 1981.

(Haitian story about Teegra, a little tiger who gives his treasured banjo to his goat friend, Cabree.)

—————. *White Wave: A Chinese Tale.* Illus. by Ed Young. Crowell, 1979.

(Moon goddess assists a poor farmer. Grades 2–5.)

Yagawa, Sumiko. *The Crane Wife.* Illus. by Suekichi Akaba. Morrow, 1981.

(Japanese folktale about a peasant who marries a beautiful and mysterious woman.)

Young, Ed. *The Terrible Nung Gwama: A Chinese Folktale.* Collins-World, 1978.

(A poor young woman finds a way to avoid becoming supper for a repulsive monster. Act out and retell.)

Zemach, Harve. *Duffy and the Devil.* Illus. by Margot Zemach. Farrar, 1973.

(Uproarious English variant of *Rumpelstiltskin* by Grimm. Don't miss the wonderful Miller-Brody filmstrip, narrated with throaty perfection by Tammy Grimes. See also Ness's *Tom Tit Tot* for another rendition.)

—————. *Nail Soup: A Swedish Folk Tale.* Illus. by Margot Zemach. Follett, 1964.

(A tramp cajoles food out of a stingy old woman when he claims to be able to make soup with a mere nail. Also see Brown's *Stone Soup.*)

—————. *Too Much Nose.* Illus. by Margot Zemach. Holt, 1967.

(Italian folktale of a greedy queen who gets what she deserves. See also Hutton's version, *The Nose Tree.*)

Zemach, Margot. *It Could Always Be Worse.* Farrar, 1976.

(A poor, unfortunate man needs the rabbi's advice when he can no longer stand his overcrowded one-room hut. Sufficiently raucous for improvised drama. See also Hirsch's *Could Anything Be Worse?*)

Folk & Fairy Tales, Myths & Legends

Collections

Aesop. *Aesop's Fables*. Illus. by Heidi Holder. Viking, 1981.
(Striking illustrations embellish nine assorted tales for grades 3–6.)

————. *Aesop's Fables*. Selected by Louis Untermeyer. Illus. by Alice and Martin Provenson. Golden, 1965.
(Large, amusingly illustrated anthology for K–3. Most stories are ideal for acting out in pairs.)

————. *The Fables of Aesop*. Retold by Joseph Jacobs. Illus. by David Levine. Macmillan, 1964.
(A good collection by the noted eighteenth-century English folklorist. For all ages.)

Afanasev, Nikolaevich. *Russian Folk Tales*. Trans. by Robert Chandler. Illus. by Ivan I. Bilibin. Random, 1980.
(Seven classic stories collected by an eighteenth-century Russian folklorist and illustrated by a well-known artist of that era. Grades 3–6.)

Appiah, Peggy. *Tales of an Ashanti Father*. Illus. by Mora Dickson. Deutsch, 1967.
(Twenty-two African trickster stories from Ghana about the spiderman, Kwaku Ananse, and other characters. Grades 3–6.)

Arkhurst, Joyce Cooper. *The Adventures of Spider: West African Folktales*. Illus. by Jerry Pinkney. Little, 1964.
(Six good-natured stories from Liberia and Ghana. Don't miss reading aloud the mood-setting introduction. Grades 1–4.)

Arnott, Kathleen. *Animal Folk Tales Around the World*. Illus. by Bernadette Watts. Walck, 1970.
(Thirty-nine stories from every continent. All ages.)

Asbjornsen, Peter Christen, and Moe, Jorgen. *Norwegian Folk Tales*. Trans. by Pat Shaw Iversen and Carl Norman. Illus. by Erik Werenskiold and Theodor Kittelsen. Viking, 1960.
(Three dozen tales collected by the famous eighteenth-century Norwegian folklorists. Grades 4–6.)

Bang, Molly. *The Goblins Giggle*. Scribner, 1973.
(Five chillers from Japan, Ireland, Germany, France, and China. Grades 3–6.)

Benson, Sally. *Stories of the Gods and Heroes*. Illus. by Steele Savage. Dial, 1940.

(Over twenty mostly familiar Greek and Roman myths, using Roman names. Grades 4–6.)

Brooke, L. Leslie. *The Golden Goose Book*. Warne, 1905.
(The title tale and three other well-known stories: "The Three Bears," "The Three Little Pigs," and "Tom Thumb." Grades K–3.)

Carle, Eric. *Twelve Tales from Aesop*. Philomel, 1980.
(Old favorites retold. Short and sweet for reenacting. Grades K–2.)

Carlson, Natalie Savage. *King of the Cats and Other Tales*. Illus. by David Frampton. Doubleday, 1980.
(Folktales about such legendary creatures as a lutin, a Korrigan, and a Loup Garou, all from the Brittany province of France. Grades 3–6.)

Chase, Richard. *Grandfather Tales*. Illus. by Berkeley Williams, Jr. Houghton, 1948.
(Sensational American-English folk tales collected by the author in North Carolina, Virginia, and Kentucky. Grades K–6, depending on the individual story.)

—————. *Jack Tales*. Illus. by Berkeley Williams, Jr. Houghton, 1943.
(Southern Appalachian folktales about clever Jack, alternately lazy and hardworking, as he seeks his fortune from kings, farmers, and giants. Grades 4–6.)

Climo, Shirley. *Piskies, Spriggans, and Other Magical Beings: Tales from the Droll-Teller*. Illus. by Joyce Audy dos Santos. Crowell, 1981.
(All about supernatural types from Cornwall, England. Grades 3–6.)

Coatsworth, Emerson and David. *The Adventures of Nanabush: Ojibway Indian Stories*. Illus. by Francis Kagige. Atheneum, 1980.
(How the great magician created and improved the world. Grades 2–5.)

Courlander, Harold, and Herzog, George. *The Cow-Tail Switch and Other West African Stories*. Illus. by Madye Lee Chastain. Holt, 1947.
(Marvelous for reading and telling. Grades 2–6.)

—————. *The Hat-Shaking Dance and Other Tales from the Gold Coast*. Illus. by Enrico Arno. Harcourt, 1957.
(About Anansi the Spider and others, told by the Ashanti people of Ghana. Grades 2–6.)

—————. *The Piece of Fire and Other Haitian Tales*. Illus. by Beth and Joe Krush. Harcourt, 1942.

(Includes many whimsical tales of Bouki, a trickster and fool. Grades 3–6.)

Cox, Miriam. *The Magic and the Sword: The Greek Myths Retold*. Illus. by Harold Price. Harper, 1962.
(Familiar myths, including the travels of Ulysses. Grades 4–6.)

Credle, Ellis. *Tall Tales from the High Hills*. Illus. by Richard Bennett. Nelson, 1957.
(Droll whoppers from the Blue Ridge Mountains. Grades 4–6.)

D'Aulaire, Ingri and Edgar Parin. *Ingri and Edgar Parin d'Aulaire's Book of Greek Myths*. Doubleday, 1962.
(Large, attractive compilation of stories about the gods and goddesses. Grades 4–6.)

Deutsch, Babette, and Yarmolinsky, Avrahm. *More Tales of Faraway Folk*. Illus. by Janina Domanska. Harper, 1963.
(Fifteen short tales from remote nothern regions of the Soviet Union and from Finland. Grades 1–3.)
—————. *Tales of Faraway Folk*. Illus. by Irena Lorentowicz. Harper, 1952.
(Ten brief tales from distant northern regions of the Soviet Union. Grades 1–3.)

Edmonds, I.G. *Trickster Tales*. Illus. by Sean Morrison. Lippincott, 1966.
(Eighteen cunning characters from around the globe. Grades 3–6.)

Feuerlicht, Roberta. *The Legends of Paul Bunyan*. Illus. by Kurt Werth. Collier, 1966.
(Tall tales of the legendary U.S. logger and his blue ox, Babe. Grades 3–6.)

Finger, Charles. *Tales from Silver Lands*. Illus. by Paul Honore. Doubleday, 1924.
(Nineteen stories told by the Indians of South America. A Newbery Award winner. Grades 3–6.)

Galdone, Paul. *Three Aesop Fox Fables*. Seabury, 1971.
(Fox has dealings with grapes, a stork, and a cheese-carrying crow. Grades K–2.)

Gates, Doris. *Lord of the Sky: Zeus*. Illus. by Robert Handville. Viking, 1972.
(Greek myths about the father of the gods and his influence over mortals and immortals alike. Grades 5–6.)
—————. *The Warrior Goddess: Athena*. Illus. by Don Bolognese. Viking, 1972.
(Greek myths about Pallas Athena and the mortals she assists. Grades 5–6.)

Ginsburg, Mirra. *The Lazies*. Illus. by Marian Parry. Macmillan, 1973.
(Short yarns of Russian fools and do-nothings. Grades 2–4.)
——————. *Three Rolls and One Doughnut*. Illus. by Anita Lobel. Dial, 1970.
(Funny Russian fables. All ages.)
Greene, Ellin. *Clever Cooks: A Concoction of Stories, Charms, Recipes and Riddles*. Illus. by Trina Schart Hyman. Lothrop, 1973.
(A dozen food-related folktales starring quick-witted chefs, both male and female. Grades 2–5.)
Grimm, Jacob. *The Brothers Grimm Popular Folk Tales*. Trans. by Brian Alderson. Illus. by Michael Foreman. Doubleday, 1978.
(Appealing collection of 31 mostly familiar stories. All ages.)
——————. *Fairy Tales of the Brothers Grimm*. Illus. by Kay Nielsen. Viking, 1979.
(Twelve stories grace this facsimile edition, originally published in 1925. Grades 2–5.)
——————. *Grimm's Fairy Tales: 20 Stories*. Illus. by Arthur Rackham. Viking, 1973.
(Facsimile of the beautiful early-twentieth-century edition. Grades 3–6.)
——————. *The Juniper Tree, and Other Tales from Grimm*. Trans. by Lore Segal and Randall Jarrell. Illus. by Maurice Sendak. Farrar, 1973.
(Two handsome volumes, including many of the Grimms' lesser-known and more melancholy sagas. Grades 3–6.)
——————. *More Tales from Grimm*. Illus. by Wanda Gag. Coward, 1947.
——————. *Tales from Grimm*. Illus. by Wanda Gag. Coward, 1936.
(Two above are marvelous collections of tales. All ages.)
Hardendorff, Jeanne. *Tricky Peik and Other Picture Tales*. Illus. by Tomie de Paola. Lippincott, 1967.
(A group of twenty brief international stories, amusing and ripe for retelling. Grades K–3.)
Harper, Wilhelmina. *Ghosts and Goblins: Stories for Halloween*. Illus. by William Wiesner. Dutton, 1965.
(Anthology of traditional chillers. Grades 2–5.)
Harris, Christie. *Mouse Woman and the Mischief-Makers*. Illus. by Douglas Tait. Atheneum, 1977.

————. *Mouse Woman and the Muddleheads*. Illus. by Douglas Tait. Atheneum, 1979.

————. *Mouse Woman and the Vanished Princesses*. Illus. by Douglas Tait. Atheneum, 1976.
(Entertaining Northwest Coastal Indian stories of the tiny supernatural narnauk grandmother who comes to the aid of young people in trouble. Grades 4–6.)

————. *Once Upon a Totem*. Illus. by John Frazer Mills. Atheneum, 1966.

————. *The Trouble with Adventurers*. Illus. by Douglas Tait. Atheneum, 1982.

————. *The Trouble with Princesses*. Illus. by Douglas Tait. Atheneum, 1980.
(A variety of fascinating Northwest Coast Indian legends of the Eagle, Raven, Bear, and Wolf clans. Grades 4–6.)

Haviland, Virginia. *The Fairy Tale Treasury*. Illus. by Raymond Briggs. Coward, 1972.
(Large format, delightful illustrations and over thirty stories. Grades K–3.)

————. *Favorite Fairy Tales Told in Czechoslovakia*. Illus. by Trina Schart Hyman. Little, 1966.

————. *Favorite Fairy Tales Told in Denmark*. Illus. by Margot Zemach. Little, 1971.

————. *Favorite Fairy Tales Told in England*. Illus. by Bettina. Little, 1959.

————. *Favorite Fairy Tales Told in France*. Illus. by Roger DuVoisin. Little, 1959.

————. *Favorite Fairy Tales Told in Greece*. Illus. by Nonny Hogrogian. Little, 1970.

————. *Favorite Fairy Tales Told in India*. Illus. by Blair Lent. Little, 1973.

————. *Favorite Fairy Tales Told in Ireland*. Illus. by Artur Marokvia. Little, 1961.

————. *Favorite Fairy Tales Told in Italy*. Illus. by Evaline Ness. Little, 1965.

————. *Favorite Fairy Tales Told in Japan*. Illus. by George Suyeoka. Little, 1967.

————. *Favorite Fairy Tales Told in Norway*. Illus. by Leonard Weisgard. Little, 1961.

————. *Favorite Fairy Tales Told in Russia*. Illus. by Herbert Danska. Little, 1961.

————. *Favorite Fairy Tales Told in Scotland*. Illus. by Adrienne Adams. Little, 1963.

————. *Favorite Fairy Tales Told in Spain*. Illus. by Barbara Cooney. Little, 1963.

—————. *Favorite Fairy Tales Told in Sweden.* Illus. by Ronni Solbert. Little, 1966.
(Distinguished folklorist retells five tales in each of these splendid national collections. Grades K–4.)

—————. *North American Legends.* Illus. by Ann Strugnell. Collins, 1979.
(Traditional American stories of Indians, Eskimos, European immigrants, and black Americans. Grades 4–6.)

Hoke, Helen. *Witches, Witches, Witches.* Illus. by W. R. Lohse. Watts, 1958.
(Spooky tales for October 31. Grades 1–5.)

Hopkins, Lee Bennett. *A-Haunting We Will Go: Ghostly Stories and Poems.* Illus. by Vera Rosenberry. Whitman, 1977.

—————. *Monsters, Ghoulies and Creepy Creatures: Fantastic Tales and Poems.* Illus. by Vera Rosenberry. Whitman, 1977.

—————. *Witching Time: Mischievous Stories and Poems.* Illus. by Vera Rosenberry. Whitman, 1977.
(Three above are collections of folktales, poems, and contemporary spine-tinglers. Grades 2–4.)

Hunter, Molly. *A Furl of Fairy Wind.* Illus. by Stephen Gammell. Harper, 1977.
(Four lovely lyrical tales by the gifted Scottish author. Grades 3–6.)

Jagendorf, M.A., and Weng, Virginia. *The Magic Boat and Other Chinese Folk Stories.* Illus. by Wan-go Weng. Vanguard, 1980.
(Large collection representing the many ethnic groups in China. All ages.)

Jaquith, Priscilla. *Bo Rabbit Smart for True: Folktales from the Gullah.* Illus. by Ed Young. Philomel, 1981.
(African-based animal tales from the Sea Islands of Georgia and South Carolina. All ages.)

Kendall, Carol, and Li, Yao-wen. *Sweet and Sour: Tales from China.* Illus. by Shirley Felts. Seabury, 1979.
(Twenty-four stories from ancient China. Grades 3–6.)

Lang, Andrew. *The Blue Fairy Book.* Illus. by Antony Maitland. Viking, 1978.

—————. *The Green Fairy Book.* Illus. by Antony Maitland. Viking, 1978.

—————. *The Pink Fairy Book.* Illus. by Colin McNaughton. Viking, 1982.

—————. *The Red Fairy Book.* Illus. by Faith Jaques. Viking, 1976.

—————. *The Yellow Fairy Book*. Illus. by Erik Blegvad. Viking, 1980.
(Five from the marvelous series of "color" collections of international folktales, originally compiled in the late-nineteenth century and reissued. Edited by Brian Alderson. All ages.)

Leach, Maria. *Noodles, Nitwits and Numskulls*. Illus. by Kurt Werth. World, 1961.
(Brief tales of fools the world over. All ages.)

—————. *The Rainbow Book of American Folk Tales and Legends*. Illus. by Marc Simont. World, 1958.
(Oversized format includes tall tales, state lore, bad men, scary stories, local legends, and then some. Grades 3–6.)

—————. *The Thing at the Foot of the Bed*. Illus. by Kurt Werth. World, 1959.
(Three dozen short, ghostly folktales. Get out a candle, turn off the lights, and practice your screams. Grades 2–6.)

—————. *Whistle in the Graveyard: Folktales to Chill Your Bones*. Illus. by Ken Rinciardi. Viking, 1974.
(Over three dozen brief ghost stories. Grades 4–6.)

Lester, Julius. *The Knee-High Man and Other Tales*. Illus. by Ralph Pinto. Dial, 1972.
(Six marvelous black American folktales, perfect for telling. All ages.)

Lurie, Alison. *Clever Gretchen, and Other Forgotten Folktales*. Illus. by Margot Tomes. Crowell, 1980.
(Fifteen tales of resourceful European heroines. Grades 4–6.)

Manning-Sanders, Ruth. *A Book of Spooks and Spectres*. Illus. by Robin Jacques. Dutton, 1979.
(One of a terrific series of collected creature folktales, including *A Book of Monsters/Witches/Giants/Sorcerers and Spells*, to name just a few of the more than fifteen titles by Manning-Sanders. Grades 2–6.)

McCormick, Dell J. *Paul Bunyan Swings His Axe*. Caxton, 1936.
(Tall tales of the famous U.S. logger, illustrated by the author. Grades 3–6.)

Melzack, Ronald. *Raven, Creator of the World*. Illus. by Laszlo Gal. Little, 1970.
(Eskimo legends about the supernatural man-bird and how he formed the world. For more "Raven" tales, see Gail Robinson's *Raven the Trickster*. Grades 3–6.)

Mendoza, George. *The Crack in the Wall, & Other Terribly Weird Tales*. Illus. by Mercer Mayer. Dial, 1968.

—————. *Gwot! Horribly Funny Hairticklers*. Illus. by Steven Kellogg. Harper, 1967.
(Two collections of tales that appeal to those who love feeling squeamish. Grades 2–4.)

Minard, Rosemary. *Womenfolk and Fairy Tales*. Illus. by Suzanne Klein. Houghton, 1975.
(From the Chinese Red Riding Hoods to Kate Crackernuts, these female protagonists save the day. Grades 3–6.)

Picard, Barbara Leonie. *The Faun and the Woodcutter's Daughter*. Illus. by Charles Stewart. Criterion, 1964.
(Delightful original fairy tales. Grades 4–6.)

Price, Margaret Evans. *Myths and Enchantment Tales*. Illus. by Evelyn Urbanowich. Rand, 1960.
(Assorted Greek myths, using mostly Roman names. Grades 4–6.)

Protter, Eric. *A Children's Treasury of Folk and Fairy Tales*. Beaufort, 1982.
(Over three dozen enchanting European stories. All ages.)

Rice, Eve. *Once in a Wood: Ten Tales from Aesop*. Greenwillow, 1979.
(Familiar fables, ideal for acting out in pairs or small groups. Grades K–2.)

Robinson, Adjai. *Singing Tales of Africa*. Illus. by Christine Price. Scribner, 1974.
(The musical refrains for each of these seven stories are included for you to learn and use with the tales. Grades 1–4.)

Robinson, Gail. *Raven the Trickster: Legends of the North American Indians*. Illus. by Joanna Troughton. Atheneum, 1982.
(How Raven, the creator of the world, weaves in and out of trouble. Grades 4–6.)

Robinson, Gail, and Hill, Douglas. *Coyote the Trickster*. Illus. by Graham McCallum. Crane Russak, 1976.
(North American Indian legends about troublemaking heroes including Coyote, Raven, and Fox. Grades 4–6.)

Rockwell, Anne. *The Old Woman and Her Pig and 10 Other Stories*. Crowell, 1979.

—————. *The Three Bears & 15 Other Stories*. Crowell, 1975.
(Two collections of well-known tales, illuminated with bright watercolors on every page. Grades K–2.)

Rounds, Glen. *Ol' Paul, the Mighty Logger*. Holiday, 1976. ("Being a True Account of the Seemingly Incredible Exploits and Inventions of the Great Paul Bunyan." Reissued on the fortieth anniversary of the original publication. Grades 4–6.)

Sadler, Catherine Edwards. *Treasure Mountain: Folktales from Southern China*. Illus. by Cheng Mung Yun. Atheneum, 1982.
(Six captivating stories for grades 4–6.)

Schwartz, Alvin. *Scary Stories To Tell in the Dark*. Illus. by Stephen Gammell. Lippincott, 1981.
(Don't forget your flashlight. Includes terrifying illustrations. Grades 4–6.)

————. *Whoppers: Tall Tales and Other Lies*. Illus. by Glen Rounds. Lippincott, 1975.
(As fine a collection of ranting bunkum a liar could assemble from American folklore. Grades 3–5.)

Schwartz, Howard. *Elijah's Violin and Other Jewish Fairy Tales*. Illus. by Linda Heller. Harper, 1983.
(Impressive compilation from Eastern Europe, Palestine, the Middle East, and even India, some dating from the fifth century. Grades 4–6.)

Singer, Isaac Bashevis. *When Shlemiel Went to Warsaw & Other Stories*. Illus. by Margot Zemach. Farrar, 1979.
(Jewish folktales and original stories by a master of Yiddish literature. Grades 4–6.)

————. *Zlateh the Goat and Other Stories*. Illus. by Maurice Sendak. Harper, 1966.
(Both the foolish and the unfortunate prevail in these lustrous folklore-based Yiddish stories. Grades 4–6.)

Stoutenburg, Adrien. *American Tall Tales*. Illus. by Richard M. Powers, Viking, 1966.
(Includes one chapter for each of eight heroes including Pecos Bill, Mike Fink and Stormalong. Grades 3–5.)

Tashjian, Virginia A. *Once There Was and Was Not*. Illus. by Nonny Hogrogian. Little, 1966.
(Wonderful Armenian tales. Grades 2–6.)

————. *Three Apples Fell from Heaven*. Illus. by Nonny Hogrogian. Little, 1971.
(More wonderful Armenian tales. Grades 2–6.)

Uchida, Yoshiko. *The Magic Listening Cap: More Folk Tales from Japan*. Harcourt, 1955.
(Fourteen stories for grades 2–4.)

————. *The Sea of Gold and Other Tales from Japan*. Illus. by Marianne Yamaguchi. Gregg, 1980.

(Twelve spellbinding stories. Grades 3–6.)

Vuong, Lynette Dyer. *The Brocaded Slipper and Other Vietnamese Tales*. Illus. by Vo-Dinh Mai. Addison, 1982.
(Five tales reminiscent of Cinderella, Tom Thumb, Rip Van Winkle, and other familiar characters. Grades 3–6.)

Walker, Barbara. *Once There Was and Twice There Wasn't*. Illus. by Gordon Kibbee. Follett, 1968.
(Turkish tales of the bald-headed peasant boy, Keloglan. Grades 2–4.)

—————. *Watermelons, Walnuts, and the Wisdom of Allah and Other Tales of the Hoca*. Illus. by Harold Berson. Parents, 1967.
(Eighteen whimsical stories about Nasreddin Hoca, the Turkish religious leader and consummate fool. Grades 2–5.)

White, Anne Terry. *The Golden Treasury of Myths and Legends*. Illus. by Alice and Martin Provenson. Golden, 1959.
(Exciting tales of the Greeks, Vikings, Celts, Persians, and French. Grades 4–6.)

Withers, Carl. *I Saw a Rocket Walk a Mile: Nonsense Tales, Chants and Songs from Many Lands*. Illus. by John E. Johnson. Holt, 1965.
(Chock-full of short, tellable ditties. Grades K–3.)

—————. *A World of Nonsense: Strange and Humorous Tales from Many Lands*. Illus. by John E. Johnson. Holt, 1968.
(Fifty silly tall tales and numskull stories. Grades 1–5.)

Wolkstein, Diane. *Lazy Stories*. Illus. by James Marshall. Seabury, 1976.
(Three funny ones from Japan, Mexico, and Laos. Includes helpful notes for the storyteller. Grades 1–4.)

—————. *The Magic Orange Tree and Other Haitian Folktales*. Illus. by Elsa Henriquez. Knopf, 1978.
(Fascinating stories collected in Haiti by Wolkstein, who has appended excellent storytellers' notes and music for each tale. Grades 1–6.)

First two stanzas of "The Queen of Eene" by Jack Prelutsky and accompanying illustration by Victoria Chess from THE QUEEN OF EENE by Jack Prelutsky. Text copyright © 1970, 1978 by Jack Prelutsky. Illustration copyright © 1978 by Victoria Chess. Reproduced by permission of Greenwillow Books (A Division of William Morrow & Company).

Using Poetry and Other Nonsensical Non-Fiction

Children's poetry is hard to resist, especially when you start by reading such zanies as Shel Silverstein, Kaye Starbird, Jack Prelutsky, and William Cole. Yet many teachers and librarians avoid poetry like chicken pox; we know it's there, but if we don't encourage it, perhaps we can get away with using only what's in the basals. Otherwise learned adults are under the grand delusion that children hate poetry and would rather avoid it, but children who avoid it just haven't heard any lately. Who could withstand the dulcet charms of:

> The Queen of Eene is such a goose,
> She brushed her teeth with onion juice.
> And then she said, "I do not see
> Why people do not visit me."
> (from *The Queen of Eene* by Jack Prelutsky)

Listen to students jumping rope and bouncing balls, and you'll hear traces of the chants from your own childhood, passed down intact from one generation to another. Books by Alvin Schwartz and Duncan Emrich are compilations of all the rhythms, superstitions, sayings, and riddles of childhood, and children devour these collections. They love the sound and cadence of nonsense, even if they don't really understand all of it.

Poetry is becoming publicly respectable once again, as evinced by Shel Silverstein's *A Light in the Attic*, number one on the *New York Times* Best Seller List for much of 1982. This was the first time a children's book had ever even made the top ten. That book and its partner *Where the Sidewalk Ends* have gotten much deserved notice, but don't ignore all those other alluring collections that did not garner such popular acclaim. Start with funny, short poems, work up to longer epic ones, and then read some to make your students pensive or even teary.

There's no point in suggesting individual poems for you to sample because taste in poetry is so personal. Grab some books from the list and dive in; read aloud those you like, and turn the page on those you don't. Often you will stumble upon a poem that fits perfectly with a folktale or fiction book that you plan to read. Don't trust your memory—make a copy of the poem and record where you found it—immediately, before it slips your mind. Actually, you'll probably end up memorizing your favorites, as I did when I heard Dennis Lee's manic and gory recitation of "Bloody Bill" on his Caedmon record, *Alligator Pie*. (I transcribed it from the record immediately upon hearing it, mumbling fiendishly all the while, and learned it "tout de suite.")

Sure, children dislike memorizing poetry—if it's ninety-six stanzas long and you require a formal recitation as part of their reading grade. But throw a poetry gala after everyone picks a favorite poem and memorizes it, serve Alligator Pie or other such rhyme-based tidbits, and see how the reciters love to perform. Denude the poetry section of the library; pick a peck of pickled poems on all subjects both serious and silly, tongue twisters (Oh, how students love to write those!), knock-knock jokes, and riddles, and watch your new-found poets and nonsense-mongers sprout. Write your own limericks, trade antique elephant jokes and superstitions, practice your puns, act out narrative poems, and let language arts lift everybody's spirits for the rest of the year.

Poetry and Other Nonsensical Non-Fiction

Adler, David A., comp. *The Carsick Zebra and Other Animal Riddles.* Illus. by Tomie de Paola. Holiday, 1983.
("Which dogs make the best librarians? Hush puppies." And other amusing ones. Grades K–3.)

Adoff, Arnold. *Eats.* Illus. by Susan Russo. Lothrop, 1979.
(Food poems for those who love to indulge. Read a few before lunch. All ages.)

Agree, Rose H., comp. *How To Eat a Poem & Other Morsels: Food Poems for Children.* Illus. by Peggy Wilson. Pantheon, 1967.
(A collection divided into edible categories. See also Adoff's *Eats* and Cole's *Poem Stew.* All ages.)

Alderson, Brian, comp. *Cakes and Custard.* Illus. by Helen Oxenbury. Morrow, 1975.
(Large lustrous collection of children's nursery rhymes. Grades K–1.)

Arbuthnot, May Hill, comp. *Time for Poetry.* Scott, Foresman, 1961.
(Large anthology of poetry for all days and moods. Includes valuable chapters with instructions for reading poetry to children and choral reading. All ages.)

Barrol, Grady. *The Little Book of Anagrams.* Illus. by Liz Victor. Harvey House, 1978.
(By rearranging letters in a word or phrase, you can create new ones. Just enough examples to get you and your students started. Grades 2–6.)

Bennett, Jill, comp. *Tiny Tim: Verses for Children.* Illus. by Helen Oxenbury. Delacorte, 1981.
(Enchantingly illustrated humorous poems, one per page, for the youngest set. Grades K–2.)

Bodecker, N.M., comp. *It's Raining Said John Twaining: Danish Nursery Rhymes.* Atheneum, 1973.
(Rhymes to chant over and over again. Grades K–1.)

—————. *Let's Marry Said the Cherry and Other Nonsense Poems.* Atheneum, 1974.
(Silly, short, good-humored verse. All ages.)

—————. *A Person from Britain Whose Head Was the Shape of a Mitten and Other Limericks.* Atheneum, 1980.
(The author's whimsical line drawings add to the cheery good humor of over four dozen limericks. Fourth graders and older will enjoy trying their hands at writing more. For

other limerick books, see also John E. Brewton's *They've Discovered a Head in the Box for the Bread*, Sara and John E. Brewton's *Laughable Limericks*, Edward Lear's *How Pleasant to Know Mr. Lear*, and Arnold Lobel's *The Book of Pigericks*. Grades 2–6.)

Brandreth, Gyles, comp. *The Biggest Tongue Twister Book in the World*. Illus. by Alex Chin. Sterling, 1978.
(An alphabetical assortment, incorporating verses from the first tongue twister book in the United States, *Peter Piper's Practical Principles of Plain and Perfect Pronunciation* and many more contemporary ones. Encourage your pupils to make up their own alliterative sentences. See also Rosenbloom's *Twist These on Your Tongue* and Schwartz's *A Twister of Twists, A Tangler of Tongues*. All ages.)

Brewton, John, and Blackburn, Lorraine A., comps. *They've Discovered a Head in the Box for the Bread and Other Laughable Limericks*. Illus. by Fernando Krahn. Crowell, 1978.
(Giggles abound. Don't miss the last section: "Write the Last Line Yourself"—a good way to ease your fourth through sixth graders into composing. For more limericks, see Bodecker's *A Person from Britain Whose Head Was the Shape of a Mitten*, Sara and John E. Brewton's *Laughable Limericks*, Edward Lear's *How Pleasant to Know Mr. Lear*, and Lobel's *The Book of Pigericks*. All ages.)

Brewton, John E., Blackburn, Lorraine A., and Blackburn, George M., comps. *In the Witch's Kitchen: Poems for Halloween*. Illus. by Harriet Barton. Crowell, 1980.
(Pleasantly spooky rhymes for K–3.)

Brewton, Sara and John E., comps. *Laughable Limericks*. Illus. by Ingrid Fetz. Crowell, 1965.
(Limericks for budding poets. See also Bodecker's *A Person from Britain . . .*, John E. Brewton's *They've Discovered a Head . . .*, Lear's *How Pleasant to Know Mr. Lear*, and Lobel's *The Book of Pigericks*. All ages.)

——————. *Shrieks at Midnight: Macabre Poems, Eerie and Humorous*. Illus. by Ellen Raskin. Crowell, 1969.
(From famous poets to unknown epitaph composers, a collection to intrigue lovers of horror. Grades 4–6.)

Brewton, Sara, Brewton, John E., and Blackburn, G. Meredith, comps. *My Tang's Tungled and Other Ridiculous Situations*. Illus. by Graham Booth. Crowell, 1973.
(Short, droll poems including some tongue twisters and

limericks, all ripe for memorizing. All ages.)

Calmenson, Stephanie, comp. *Never Take a Pig to Lunch.* Illus. by Hilary Knight. Doubleday, 1982.
(And other funny poems about animals. All ages.)

Cameron, Polly, comp. *The 2-Ton Canary & Other Nonsense Riddles.* Coward, 1965.
(Elephant jokes and the like for young gigglers. Grades K–2.)

Carlson, Bernice Wells, comp. *Listen! And Help Tell the Story.* Illus. by Burmah Burris. Abingdon, 1965.
(Using sound effects and chanting refrains, children will join in on these enticing nursery rhymes, finger plays, poems, ballads, and stories. Grades K–2.)

Churchill, E. Richard, comp. *The Six-Million Dollar Cucumber: Riddles and Fun for Children.* Illus. by Carol Nicklaus. Watts, 1976.
(Animal antics guaranteed to make you chortle. All ages.)

Ciardi, John. *Fast and Slow: Poems for Advanced Children and Beginning Parents.* Illus. by Becky Gaver. Houghton, 1975.
(Whimsical verse. Grades 2–5.)

—————. *You Read to Me, I'll Read to You.* Illus. by Edward Gorey. Lippincott, 1962.
(Easy clever poems to swap with your children. Grades K–2.)

Cole, William, comp. *Beastly Boys and Ghastly Girls.* Illus. by Tomi Ungerer. World, 1964.
(Nimble-witted poems, of and for obnoxious kids. All ages.)

—————. *Dinosaurs and Beasts of Yore.* Illus. by Susanna Natti. Philomel, 1979.
(Poetry of the prehistoric. Grades 1–4.)

—————. *Good Dog Poems.* Illus. by Ruth Sanderson. Scribner, 1981.
(Anthology for lovers of mutts, thoroughbreds, and pups in between. Grades 3–6.)

—————. *I Went to the Animal Fair.* Illus. by Colette Rosselli. World, 1958.
(Animal poems for the very young. Grades K–1.)

—————. *I'm Mad at You.* Illus. by George MacClain. Collins, 1978.
(When your students are feeling cranky, read them some poems from this book. All ages.)

—————. *Oh, How Silly.* Illus. by Tomi Ungerer. Viking, 1970.

————. *Oh, Such Foolishness.* Illus. by Tomie de Paola. Lippincott, 1978.

————. *Oh, That's Ridiculous.* Illus. by Tomi Ungerer. Viking, 1972.

(Three above are collections of nonsense poems for times of general hilarity. All ages.)

————. *Poem Stew.* Illus. by Karen Weinhaus. Lippincott, 1981.

(For gourmets and fast food junkies alike; poems to tickle your appetite. If you're still hungry, try Adoff's *Eats* and Agree's *How to Eat a Poem & Other Morsels.* All ages.)

————. *The Poetry of Horses.* Illus. by Ruth Sanderson. Scribner, 1979.

(A sturdy compilation of narrative poems about riders and their equine companions. Grades 4–6.)

Corrin, Sara and Stephen, comps. *Once Upon a Rhyme: 101 Poems for Young Children.* Illus. by Jill Bennett. Faber, 1982.

(Enough to appease all the fancies that await tickling. Grades K–3.)

De Paola, Tomie, illus. *The Comic Adventures of Old Mother Hubbard and Her Dog.* Harcourt, 1981.

(Famous early-nineteenth-century nursery rhyme with de Paola's whimsical illustrations. See also versions illustrated by Evaline Ness and Paul Galdone. At the end of each verse, let students supply the rhyming word. Read again and act it out, with the children playing the dog. Grades K–1.)

Doty, Roy, comp. *Gunga Your Din-Din Is Ready: Son of Puns, Gags, Quips and Riddles.* Doubleday, 1976.

————. *King Midas Has a Gilt Complex.* Doubleday, 1978.

————. *Pinocchio Was Nosy: Grandson of Puns, Gags, Quips and Riddles.* Doubleday, 1977.

————. *Puns, Gags, Quips and Riddles: A Collection of Dreadful Jokes.* Doubleday, 1974.

————. *Q's Are Weird O's: More Puns, Gags, Quips and Riddles.* Doubleday, 1975.

————. *Tinkerbell Is a Ding-a-ling.* Doubleday, 1980.

(These six have more than enough corny jokes to satisfy even the most dented sense of humor. Grades 4–6.)

Eliot, T.S. *Old Possum's Book of Practical Cats.* Illus. by Edward Gorey. Harcourt, 1982.

(The Rum Tum Tugger, Old Deuteronomy, and Skimbleshanks are some of the felines cavorting through the poems that inspired the Broadway musical *Cats*. Grades 4–6.)

Emrich, Duncan, comp. *The Hodgepodge Book.* Illus. by Ib Ohlsson. Four Winds, 1972.

—————. *The Nonsense Book.* Illus. by Ib Ohlsson. Four Winds, 1970.

—————. *The Whim-Wham Book.* Illus. by Ib Ohlsson. Four Winds, 1975.

(Three above are a browser's paradise, jam-filled with jokes, riddles, puzzles, conundrums, tongue twisters, and rhymes, all from American folklore. All ages.)

Foster, John, comp. *A First Poetry Book.* Illus. by Chris Orr, Martin White, and Joseph Wright. Oxford, 1979.

(Poems of everyday life. Grades K–2.)

Galdone, Paul, illus. *Old Mother Hubbard and Her Dog.* McGraw, 1960.

(Complete text of well-known nursery rhyme of the dame's dotty dog. See also versions illustrated by Tomie de Paola and Evaline Ness. Grades K–1.)

Garson, Eugenia, comp. *The Laura Ingalls Wilder Songbook.* Illus. by Garth Williams. Harper, 1968.

(Songs mentioned in the texts of the eight "Little House" books. With piano and guitar arrangements and notes relating each tune to the book in which it was sung. Grades 2–5.)

Gerler, William R., comp. *A Pack of Riddles.* Illus. by Giulio Maestro. Dutton, 1975.

(One riddle per page. Grades K–2.)

Glazer, Tom, comp. *Do Your Ears Hang Low? Fifty More Musical Fingerplays.* Illus. by Mila Lazarevich. Doubleday, 1980.

—————. *Eye Winker, Chin Chopper: Fifty Musical Fingerplays.* Illus. by Ron Himler. Doubleday, 1973.

(Two above present nursery songs and other clever ditties, to be performed with actions as described in the text. Grades K–2.)

—————. *Tom Glazer's Treasury of Folk Songs.* Illus. by Art Seiden. Grosset, 1964.

(Over one hundred popular folksongs for all occasions. All ages.)

Goldberg, Rube. *The Best of Rube Goldberg.* Comp. by Charles Keller. Prentice, 1979.

(Ingenious and elaborate mechanical inventions of such

necessities as a self-working corkscrew, self-shining shoes, and many more. Show each illustration as you read the instructions aloud. Because of the detail on each page, you may want to try the opaque projector. Students will certainly clamor to devise their own labor-saving devices. Grades 3–6.)

Gounaud, Karen Jo, comp. *A Very Mice Joke Book.* Illus. by Lynn Munsinger. Houghton, 1981.
(Mouse puns and riddles, decked out with mouse-terful illustrations. Let your class mouse-ter up some new ones. All ages.)

Greenfield, Eloise. *Honey, I Love.* Illus. by Diane and Leo Dillon. Crowell, 1978.
(A young black girl's poems about her world and the people in it. Grades 2–6.)

Hart, Jane, comp. *Singing Bee! A Collection of Favorite Children's Songs.* Illus. by Anita Lobel. Lothrop, 1982.
(One hundred and twenty-five mostly well-known tunes for young children, accompanied by large, beautiful illustrations, many in color. Grades K–2.)

Hoban, Russell. *Egg Thoughts and Other Frances Songs.* Illus. by Lillian Hoban. Harper, 1972.
(After reading aloud Hoban's "Frances" books about the homey adventures of the versifying young badger, try a few of her original poems. Perhaps your children will want to set them to music. Grades K–2.)

Hopkins, Lee Bennett, comp. *I Am the Cat.* Illus. by Linda Rochester Richards. Harcourt, 1981.
(A sensitive collection of cat-based poems, laced with elegant cross-hatched line drawings. All ages.)

—————. *Moments: Poems about the Seasons.* Illus. by Michael Hague. Harcourt, 1980.
(Divided into autumn, winter, spring, and summer; fifty poems by well-known poets. All ages.)

Hopkins, Lee Bennett, and Arenstein, Misha, comps. *Thread One to a Star: A Book of Poems.* Four Winds, 1976.
(Of seasons, people, cities, and personal feelings, interspersed with fittingly stark photographs. Grades 4–6.)

Hughes, Langston. *Don't You Turn Back.* Selected by Lee Bennett Hopkins. Illus. by Ann Grifalconi. Knopf, 1969.
(Short treasures expressing dreams and despair, by the famous black poet. Grades 3–6.)

Ivimey, John W. *Complete Version of Yee Three Blind Mice.* Illus. by Walton Corbould. Warne, 1979.

(First published in 1904, being the whole riotous account of how they lost their tails and got them back again. Read or sing with grades K–1.)

John, Timothy, comp. *The Great Song Book.* Illus. by Tomi Ungerer. Benn, 1978.
(Charmingly illustrated collection of over sixty well-known folk songs. All ages.)

Keller, Charles, comp. *Ballpoint Bananas and Other Jokes for Kids.* Illus. by David Barrios. Prentice, 1973.
——————. *More Ballpoint Bananas.* Illus. by Leonard Shortall. Prentice, 1977.
(Two books filled with riddles, rhymes, Tom Swifties, perverted proverbs, and other ticklish situations. All ages.)
——————. *Llama Beans.* Illus. by Dennis Nolan. Prentice, 1979.
(More dumb animal jokes with wonderfully goofy illustrations. Grades 1–4.)
——————. *The Nutty Joke Book.* Illus. by Jean-Claude Suares. Prentice, 1978.
(Riddles about peanuts and other unsuspecting nuts. All ages.)

Keller, Charles, and Baker, Richard. *The Star-Spangled Banana and Other Revolutionary Riddles.* Illus. by Tomie de Paola. Prentice, 1974.
(Bet you never realized colonial history was so funny. Lighten up those social studies lessons. Grades 2–6.)

Kennedy, X.J., comp. *Knock at a Star: A Child's Introduction to Poetry.* Illus. by Karen Ann Weinhaus. Little, 1982.
(Brief nuggets of poems and advice on how to appreciate them. Includes numerous suggestions for the reluctant teacher. Grades 4–6.)
——————. *One Winter Night in August and Other Nonsense Jingles.* Illus. by David McPhail. Atheneum, 1975.
——————. *The Phantom Ice Cream Man: More Nonsense Verse.* Illus. by David McPhail. Atheneum, 1979.
(Two slim volumes of short, spirited poetic absurdities. All ages.)

Larrick, Nancy, comp. *Piper, Pipe That Song Again: Poems for Boys and Girls.* Illus. by Kelly Oechsli. Random, 1965.
(A pleasant assortment for grades K–2.)

Lear, Edward. *How Pleasant to Know Mr. Lear.* Selected and with notes by Myra Cohn Livingston. Holiday, 1982.
(Insightful glimpse into the poetry, life, and illustrations of the grand master of limericks. For additional limericks by

Lear and others, see also Bodecker's *A Person from Britain . . .*, Brewton's *They've Discovered a Head . . .* and *Laughable Limericks,* and Lobel's *The Book of Pigericks.* Grades 4–6.)

Lee, Dennis. *Alligator Pie.* Illus. by Frank Newfeld. Houghton, 1974.

——————. *Garbage Delight.* Illus. by Frank Newfeld. Houghton, 1977.

——————. *Nicholas Knock and Other People.* Illus. by Frank Newfeld. Houghton, 1974.

(Three above contain delightfully galloping nonsense poems, mostly for grades K–2, with a few for the older grades thrown in, too.)

Leonard, Marcia, comp. *Cricket's Jokes, Riddles & Other Stuff.* Designed by John Grandits. Random, 1977.

(The usual assortment. If your students are not familiar with *Cricket* magazine, it's never too late to make introductions. All ages.)

Lewis, Richard, comp. *Miracles: Poems by Children of the English-Speaking World.* Simon & Schuster, 1966.

(Exquisite examples of children's creative endeavors. All ages.)

Livingston, Myra Cohn, comp. *Callooh! Callay! Holiday Poems for Young Readers.* Illus. by Janet Stevens. Atheneum, 1980.

(Of New Year's Day to Christmas Eve, and all the major holidays in between; several poems for each. All ages.)

Lobel, Arnold. *The Book of Pigericks.* Harper, 1983.

(Pig limericks. Try composing your own about porkers or any other interesting beasts. For other limerick books, see also Bodecker's *A Person from Britain . . .*, Brewton's *They've Discovered a Head . . .* and *Laughable Limericks,* and Lear's *How Pleasant to Know Mr. Lear.* All ages.)

Longfellow, Henry Wadsworth. *Paul Revere's Ride.* Illus. by Paul Galdone. Crowell, 1963.

(An appropriate supplement to your colonial history lesson. Grades 3–6.)

Merriam, Eve. *Catch a Little Rhyme.* Illus. by Imero Gobbato. Atheneum, 1966.

(Brief, whimsical poems for grades K–3.)

Milne, A.A. *When We Were Very Young.* Illus. by Ernest H. Shepard. Dutton, 1924.

(Book of poems of Pooh and Christopher Robin and other fanciful folk. Grades K–3.)

Mizamura, Kazue. *Flower Moon Snow: A Book of Haiku.* Crowell, 1977.

(Delicate haiku for all ages.)

Moore, Clement C. *The Night Before Christmas.* Illus. by Tomie de Paola. Holiday, 1980.

(Saint Nick and his reindeer prance again, thanks to de Paola's jaunty watercolors. All ages.)

Moore, Lilian, comp. *Go with the Poem.* McGraw, 1979.

(Collection of fascinating introspective verse by twentieth-century poets. Grades 3–6.)

Moore, Lilian. *See My Lovely Poison Ivy and Other Verses about Witches, Ghosts and Things.* Illus. by Diane Dawson. Atheneum, 1979.

(A treat for Halloween, Friday the 13th, and other dark days. Grades K–3.)

Morrison, Lillian, comp. *Best Wishes, Amen.* Illus. by Loretta Lustig. Crowell, 1974.

——————. *Yours Till Niagara Falls.* Illus. by Marjorie Bauernschmidt. Crowell, 1950.

(Two handbooks of rhymes and sayings to write in autograph books. All ages.)

Mother Goose. *Granfa' Grig Had a Pig and Other Rhymes Without Reason from Mother Goose.* Comp. and illus. by Wallace Tripp. Little, 1976.

(A sparkling frolic through nursery rhymes both known and obscure. For additional poems and captivating illustrations, see Wallace Tripp's companion volume, *A Great Big Ugly Man Came Up and Tied His Horse to Me.* Grades K–4.)

——————. *Gray Goose and Gander & Other Mother Goose Rhymes.* Collected and illus. by Anne Rockwell. Crowell, 1980.

(Cheerful watercolors illuminate over four dozen nursery rhymes for grades K–1.)

——————. *James Marshall's Mother Goose.* Illus. by James Marshall. Farrar, 1979.

(Filled with Marshall's dizzy comic creatures. Grades K–2.)

——————. *The Real Mother Goose.* Rand, 1916.

(Grand oversized collection of more than 200 nursery rhymes for grades K–1.)

——————. *Richard Scarry's Best Mother Goose Ever.* Illus. by Richard Scarry. Golden, 1964.

(Large, boisterous double-page spreads enfold each of fifty rhymes. Grades K–1.)

Nash, Ogden. *Custard and Company*. Illus. by Quentin Blake. Little, 1980.
(Captivatingly funny rhymes, accompanied by Blake's whimsical scratches.)

Ness, Evaline, comp. *Amelia Mixed the Mustard and Other Poems*. Scribner, 1975.
(Twenty poems about females of all ages and types. All ages.)

—————, illus. *Old Mother Hubbard and Her Dog*. Holt, 1972.
(An English sheepdog has the role in this version of the old rhyme. See also renditions by Paul Galdone and Tomie de Paola. Grades K–1.)

O'Neill, Mary L. *What Is That Sound!* Illus. by Lois Ehlert. Atheneum, 1968.
(Poems about the sounds in our lives. Make sound effects tapes to accompany the poems of your choice. All ages.)

Peck, Robert Newton. *Bee Tree and Other Stuff*. Illus. by Laura Lydecker. Walker, 1975.
(Poems and commentary of a Vermont farm childhood, by the author of the autobiographical "Soup" series. Grades 4–6.)

Phillips, Louis. *The Upside-Down Riddle Book*. Lothrop, 1982.
(Turn the book upside down to see the answer to each riddle. Grades K–2.)

Pomerantz, Charlotte. *If I Had a Paka*. Illus. by Nancy Tafuri. Greenwillow, 1981.
(Bright chantable poems using words from eleven different languages. If you supply your students with a list of words translated into, say, French or Spanish, they can compose their own. All ages.)

Prelutsky, Jack. *The Baby Uggs Are Hatching*. Illus. by James Stevenson. Greenwillow, 1982.

—————. *It's Christmas*. Illus. by Marylin Hafner. Greenwillow, 1981.

—————. *It's Halloween*. Illus. by Marylin Hafner. Greenwillow, 1981.

—————. *It's Thanksgiving*. Illus. by Marylin Hafner. Greenwillow, 1981.

—————. *Nightmares: Poems To Trouble Your Sleep*. Illus. by Arnold Lobel. Greenwillow, 1976.

—————. *The Queen of Eene*. Illus. by Victoria Chess. Greenwillow, 1978.

——————. *Rainy Rainy Saturday*. Illus. by Marylin Hafner. Greenwillow, 1980.

——————. *Rolling Harvey Down the Hill*. Illus. by Victoria Chess. Greenwillow, 1980.

——————. *The Sheriff of Rottenshot*. Illus. by Victoria Chess. Greenwillow, 1982.

——————. *The Snopp on the Sidewalk and Other Poems*. Illus. by Byron Barton. Greenwillow, 1977.

——————. *Zoo Doings*. Illus. by Paul O. Zelinsky. Greenwillow, 1983.

(If you relish a galloping rhyme, sprinkled with wit, mishap and glee, don't miss the genius of Prelutsky. Poems of holidays, horrifiers, and undefinable creatures skulk through the pages of his numerous collections, waiting to be intoned, burbled, and sung by each unsuspecting browser. All ages.)

Riley, James Whitcomb. *The Gobble-Uns'll Git You Ef You Don't Watch Out*. Illus. by Joel Schick. Lippincott, 1975. ("Little Orphant Annie" warns her charges of the dangers of being bad. Hone your down-home Indiana dialect, and invite your listeners to join in on the title refrain. Grades 3–6.)

Rosenbloom, Joseph, comp. *Biggest Riddle Book in the World*. Illus. by Joyce Behr. Sterling, 1976.

——————. *Dr. Knock-Knock's Official Knock-Knock Dictionary*. Illus. by Joyce Behr. Sterling, 1976.

——————. *The Gigantic Joke Book*. Illus. by Joyce Behr. Sterling, 1978.

——————. *How Do You Make an Elephant Laugh? and 699 Other Zany Riddles*. Sterling, 1979.

——————. *Monster Madness: Riddles, Jokes, Fun*. Illus. by Joyce Behr. Sterling, 1980.

——————. *Silly Verse (And Even Worse)*. Illus. by Joyce Behr. Sterling, 1979.

——————. *Sports Riddles*. Illus. by Sam Q. Weissman. Harcourt, 1982.

——————. *Twist These on Your Tongue*. Illus. by Joyce Behr. Nelson, 1978.

(Rosenbloom's manic collections of jokes, riddles, tongue twisters, rhymes, and other silliness should satisfy even the most demanding nonsense lovers. All ages.)

Sandburg, Carl. *Rainbows Are Made*. Selected by Lee Bennett Hopkins. Illus. by Fritz Eichenberg. Harcourt, 1982. (An elegant offering of poetry by the legendary American writer, accompanied with distinguished wood engravings. Grades 5–6.)

Sarnoff, Jane, and Ruffins, Reynold, comps. *Take Warning! A Book of Superstitions.* Scribner, 1978.

(An alphabetical encyclopedia of world superstitions. Students can compile their own lists. See also Alvin Schwartz's *Cross Your Fingers, Spit in Your Hat.* Grades 4–6.)

Saunders, Dennis, comp. *Magic Lights and Streets of Shining Jet.* Photos by Terry Williams. Greenwillow, 1974.

(Categorized into sections of creatures, weather and seasons, colors, and sea and shore, each one-page poem is accompanied with a color photograph on the facing page. All ages.)

Schwartz, Alvin. *Busy Buzzing Bumblebees and Other Tongue Twisters.* Illus. by Kathie Abrams. Harper, 1982.

(Fun and easy to read, with one twister per page. Grades K–2.)

————, comp. *The Cat's Elbow and Other Secret Languages.* Illus. by Margot Zemach. Farrar, 1982.

(How to speak Pig Latin, Iggity, Ku, and other coded languages for those who like to sound mysterious. Untranslated stories, riddles and rhymes are included as practice problems. Students can put their own writings in code and practice on each other. Grades 2–6.)

————. *Chin Music: Tall Talk and Other Talk, Collected from American Folklore.* Illus. by John O'Brien. Lippincott, 1979.

(Extend the vocabulary of your pupils by reading from this dictionary of colorful folk speech and have yourself a real frolication. Grades 3–6.)

————. *Cross Your Fingers, Spit in Your Hat: Superstitions and Other Beliefs.* Illus. by Glen Rounds. Lippincott, 1974.

(Witches, numbers, weather, school, and money are some of the twenty-one subjects investigated. See also Sarnoff's *Take Warning.* Grades 3–6.)

————. *Flapdoodle: Pure Nonsense from American Folklore.* Illus. by John O'Brien. Lippincott, 1980.

————. *Tomfoolery: Trickery and Foolery with Words.* Illus. by Glen Rounds. Lippincott, 1973.

————. *Witcracks: Jokes and Jests from American Folklore.* Illus. by Glen Rounds. Lippincott, 1973.

(Three similar chuckle-filled volumes of poetry, tricks, and jokes to try on unsuspecting students and friends. All ages.)

——————. *Kickle Snifters and Other Fearsome Critters, Collected from American Folklore.* Illus. by Glen Rounds. Lippincott, 1976.

(If squonks, goofus birds, and wunks are unfamiliar species, these and other peculiar animals will inspire students to make up an illustrated booklet of their own beasts. Grades 2–5.)

——————. *Ten Copycats in a Boat and Other Riddles.* Illus. by Marc Simot. Harper, 1980.

(Easy riddles from American folklore, with one per page. Grades K–2.)

——————. *A Twister of Twists, A Tangler of Tongues.* Illus. by Glen Rounds. Lippincott, 1972.

(Tie your tongue in knots with "lemon liniment," repeated five times fast, and many more. See also Brandreth's *The Biggest Tongue Twister Book in the World* and Rosenbloom's *Twist These on Your Tongue.* All ages.)

Seeger, Pete and Charles. *The Foolish Frog.* Illus. by Miloslav Jagr. Macmillan, 1973.

(Story-song about a farmer's stupendous new tune and the wild party it inspires. If you can't sing, show the merry Weston Woods filmstrip version and invite your students to join in on each chorus. Grades K–4.)

Seeger, Ruth Crawford. *American Folk Songs for Children.* Illus. by Barbara Cooney, Doubleday, 1948.

——————. *Animal Folk Songs for Children.* Illus. by Barbara Cooney. Doubleday, 1950.

(Two basic collections. The first includes an excellent guide for parents and teachers on ways to use folk songs with children. All ages.)

Seuling, Barbara. *You Can't Eat Peanuts in Church and Other Little-Known Laws.* Doubleday, 1975.

(Laughably outrageous and unbelievable laws that have been found on the books of America's towns and cities. Only the laws are listed, but surely your pupils can come up with plausible stories of what led to each one's enactment. Grades 3–5.)

Silverstein, Shel. *A Light in the Attic.* Harper, 1981.

——————. *Where the Sidewalk Ends.* Harper, 1974.

(Two of the funniest poetry books ever, illustrated with Silverstein's own whimsical line drawings. All ages.)

Smith, William Jay. *Laughing Time: Nonsense Poems.* Illus. by Fernando Krahn. Delacorte, 1980.
(Entertaining and silly, filled with beasts and a nonsense ABC. Grades K–3.)

Starbird, Kaye. *The Covered Bridge House and Other Poems.* Illus. by Jim Arnosky. Four Winds, 1979.
(A marvelous assemblage by a gifted poet. Grades 2–6.)

Tashjian, Virginia A., comp. *Juba This and Juba That: Story Hour Stretches for Large or Small Groups.* Illus. by Victoria de Larrea. Little, 1969.

————. *With a Deep Sea Smile: Story Hour Stretches for Large or Small Groups.* Illus. by Rosemary Wells. Little, 1974.
(Two spectacular collections of chants, poems, stories, fingerplays, riddles, songs, tongue twisters, and jokes. Grades K–4.)

Thaler, Mike. *The Chocolate Marshmelephant Sundae.* Watts, 1978.
(Visual jokes, riddles, puns, and other wordplays, such as a drawing of your basic peanut butter and jellyfish sandwich. Draw a few on the chalkboard for children to guess, then have them try their hands at creating new ones. Grades 3–6.)

Thayer, Ernest Lawrence. *Casey at the Bat.* Illus. by Paul Frame. Prentice, 1964.

————. *Casey at the Bat: A Ballad of the Republic, Sung in the Year 1888.* Illus. by Wallace Tripp. Coward, 1978.
(Two versions of the classic narrative poem; try reading during the tumult of World Series Week. Frame's illustrations are reminiscent of old photos, while Tripp's multicolored sketches show Casey as a pompous, uniformed bear alongside his animal teammates. Grades 4–6.)

Tripp, Wallace, comp. *A Great Big Ugly Man Came Up and Tied His Horse to Me: A Book of Nonsense Verse.* Little, 1973.
(Tripp's endearingly nutty illustrations demand closer scrutiny; when reading these goofy verses, have everyone squeeze up close. See also his *Granfa' Grig Had a Pig,* listed here under Mother Goose. Grades K–3.)

Untermeyer, Louis, comp. *The Golden Treasury of Poetry.* Illus. by Joan Walsh Anglund. Golden, 1959.
(A huge anthology, with something for every taste and occasion. All ages.)

Viorst, Judith. *If I Were in Charge of the World and Other Worries: Poems for Children and Their Parents.* Illus. by Lynne Cherry. Atheneum, 1981.
(Of wishes and worries, wicked thoughts, and facts of life for all ages.)

Wallace, Daisy, comp. *Ghost Poems.* Illus. by Tomie de Paola. Holiday, 1979.

——. *Monster Poems.* Illus. by Kay Choroa. Holiday, 1976.

——. *Witch Poems.* Illus. by Trina Schart Hyman. Holiday, 1976.
(Scary poems for Halloween and other eerie times. Grades K–4.)

Watson, Clyde. *Father Fox's Pennyrhymes.* Illus. by Wendy Watson. Crowell, 1971.
(Lovely jingling nursery-rhymish ditties. Grades K–1.)

Wilner, Isabel, comp. *The Poetry Troupe: An Anthology of Poems To Read Aloud.* Scribner, 1977.
(Comfortable whimsy-filled collection for grades K–4.)

Winn, Marie, comp. *The Fireside Book of Fun and Game Songs.* Illus. by Whitney Darrow, Jr. Simon & Schuster, 1974.
(You don't need a campfire to sing raucously; let the songs in this grand collection inspire you. All ages.)

Withers, Carl, comp. *A Rocket in My Pocket: The Rhymes and Chants of Young Americans.* Illus. by Susanne Suba. Holt, 1948.
(Rhymes, riddles, and chants for bounce ball, jump rope, spelling, counting, autograph albums, and twisted tongues, all from American folklore. Grades K–4.)

Withers, Carl, and Benet, Sula, comps. *The American Riddle Book.* Illus. by Marc Simont. Abelard, 1954.
(Over 1,000 groaners from the United States with some foreign ones to boot. Grades 2–6.)

Yolen, Jane, comp. *The Fireside Song Book of Birds and Beasts.* Illus. by Peter Parnall. Simon & Schuster, 1972.
(Animal tunes of the air, the land, the sea, and then some. All ages.)

Young, Ed, comp. *High on a Hill: A Book of Chinese Riddles.* Collins, 1980.
(Riddle-poems about animals, written in both Chinese and English, with delicately shaded pencil drawings. All ages.)

Zimmerman, Andrea Griffing, comp. *The Riddle Zoo.* Illus. by Giulio Maestro. Dutton, 1981.
(Simple, one-per-page riddles for grades K–2.)

Fifty Ways To Celebrate Books

Now that you have valiently plowed through the preceding lists, consider incorporating into your lesson plans some of the following book-related activities, designed to give a boost to any reading program. Add your own ideas to the fifty listed below and enjoy.

While book reports may range from the casual to the formal, their primary use should not be a means of checking up on students and grading them. Instead, your goal should be to get children to immerse themselves in books and to clamor for more. Books need to be part of the everyday classroom conversation, not just relegated to reading groups.

A well-balanced library program should consist of literature-based activities in addition to the traditional library skills instruction. (When I first came to Van Holten School, my aide was astonished at my request for crayons, scissors, and construction paper. After all, what did that have to do with the card catalog and the Dewey Decimal system?) In my experience, anything that excites students about books is worth the time, effort, and even the mess. Try it and see!

Discussing Books

1. Hold a panel discussion when students have read the same book or a group of similar ones.
2. Organize a pro and con debate panel, made up of those who will defend a book versus those who will criticize it. Include the author, illustrator, and publisher as characters on the panel.
3. Monitor a class discussion comparing and contrasting a well-known book (such as *The Black Stallion, The Lion, the Witch and the Wardrobe, Mrs. Frisby and the Rats of NIMH* or *Charlotte's Web*) with the movie or TV version.
4. Call individual conferences during which students talk to you about the books they are reading.
5. Have students tell the class about the book characters they would choose as best friends.
6. Everybody loves to eat. Students can devise menus for their favorite book characters and give reasons for the selections.
7. Children should each select and read aloud an interesting passage, stopping at a strategic point.
8. Students can research the lives of popular authors and

learn about their other books. *Something About the Author*, a multi-volume set edited by Anne Commire and published by Gale is a fine place to start.

9. Write a class letter to a favorite author describing your reactions to his or her books. Be flamboyant and original to ensure a response. Record a class tape, write and illustrate reactions, or send photos. Authors like some excitement in the mail.
10. Videotape individual spoken reactions to a book you are reading aloud and play it back for the class.
11. After reading aloud various authors' book dedications, have students search the library shelves for more. Then, have them compose their own, either for books they are writing or for the books that will make them famous someday.

Visualizing Books

12. For books they've read have children design their own maps of places where different characters lived or events occurred. (See the end pages of *Winnie-the-Pooh* for an example.)
13. To help visualize a book's setting, students can build miniature stage setting dioramas for climactic scenes.
14. Students can draw portraits of main characters and make construction paper picture frames for display.
15. The class can sculpt clay figures of book characters.
16. Compile a scrapbook suggested by information or events in a book you are reading aloud.
17. Make filmstrips illustrating key scenes from books, with taped narrations that children can record.

Writing About Books

18. Many books have sequels and, occasionally, even prequels. For books that have neither, children can write possible plot descriptions.
19. Students can write a character's diary, detailing memorable points from the book.
20. Have each child compose a letter that one character could have written to another.
21. Pupils can compose questions for others to answer after reading a book.
22. Have your budding lyricists compose poems or songs inspired by books they have read.
23. After reading tall tales, inspire your children to dream up their own. Compile a class book of tall tales to

share with other classes. For good copies use a scroll or several sheets taped together so that the end product will indeed be TALL.

Dramatizing Books

24. Using a flannel board, children can make felt cutouts to help tell a story.
25. Construct paper-bag or popsicle-stick puppets to use for acting out a story.
26. Break the class into groups to write skits based on episodes in books they are reading. They can rehearse their one-act plays and perform them for other classes.
27. Children love to read about other children who go to school. Spend an hour as another teacher (i.e., Miss Viola Swamp from *Miss Nelson Is Missing,* the new schoolmaster from *Farmer Boy,* or Mr. Wendell from *Fat Men from Space)* and transform your class accordingly.
28. Each student can relate a dramatic incident from the point of view of a major or minor character in the book.

Selling Books

29. Students can write and videotape TV commercials for their books. To insure diversity, discuss the many ways products are sold on the tube. These include the hard sell, the humorous spot, the slice-of-life approach, and the singing jingle.
30. Discuss the prevalence of door-to-door salespeople in the past. Children can pair up and develop door-to-door booksellers skits to sell their latest titles to the rest of the class.
31. Everyone loves to get mail. Strike up a correspondence with another class. Children can write to recommend books they love.
32. Using the *New York Times Sunday Book Review* section as an example, have your students write publishers' blurbs and reviewer quotations to sell their favorite books.
33. Children can share the most humorous incidents, the most exciting events, or their favorite sections of the books they are still reading.
34. Readers can compose telegrams. Each can attempt to give the essence of a book in a fifteen-word telegram

and in a 100-word overnight telegram. Design a ditto of a telegram or mailgram form for them to use. How about a singing telegram, for those who are musically inclined?

35. LOVE YOUR LIBRARY! Start an Ugly Book Beautification Program. After reading a dust jacket-less book, each child can create a new jacket to jazz up the cover and sell the book. Book jackets, replete with title, author, illustrator, typed spine label, book blurb on the front flap, and author information on the back flap, can then be covered with the usual plastic covers by the librarian.

36. Write book reviews for a newspaper or magazine and actually send them in for possible publication. Both *Cricket* and *Stone Soup* publish children's work.

37. Students can make radio announcements advertising books to be broadcast over the school P.A. system.

Creating Projects with Books

38. Make some book mobiles to jangle the upper spaces in your classroom. Each student can design a section. Using fiction genres as the theme, make mobiles for mystery, historical fiction, humor, sci-fi, fantasy, animals, sports, and then some, or use individual popular book characters.

39. Herald the artistic talents of your young Rembrandts when they create original illustrations to accompany stories they have just read.

40. For a "How To" book, children can make something following the directions in the book.

41. Children love tee shirts, so why not all design original ones to flaunt their books. (If rock bands and brewers can do it, why not fiction?)

42. Students can create posters advertising loved books.

43. Make a class mural to illustrate a book or books. If your ceiling is lined with acoustical tiles, decorate it with the panels you've designed on paper cut to size. When the illustration is finished, take down the tile and staple your instant Sistine ceiling to it.

Celebrating Books

44. Hold a booktalk party with popcorn and lemonade and give "coming attraction" booktalks. Raffle off your titles.

45. Try a poetry celebration for students to recite and read aloud favorite poems they have discovered.
46. Throw a costume party and have children come dressed as characters from books they have read. Give prizes, of course.
47. Hold a storytelling festival after children select and learn folktales to tell. Invite your next-door neighbors to listen.
48. Dress up as characters from well-known folktales and hold a parade. (Two teachers from my school came to the last one as a severed head on a plate from a story in Andrew Lang's *Brown Fairy Book*. They looked sensational.)

Recognizing Characters and Remembering Books

49. Play a book character guessing game. Pin 3x5 cards, each with the name of a different book character written on it, on the backs of half the class. The rest of the children act as the panel of experts. Tagged students have up to five minutes to ask yes/no questions of the panel and thus discover their characters' identities.
50. Play the "In What Book" Game. Students each write three "In What Book" questions about fiction books they've read. Try these:
    a. In what book does a girl eat only cereal, toast, and peanut butter for breakfast?
    b. In what book is a boy the only witness to the murder of his next-door neighbor?
    c. In what book does a pig refuse to give up his blanket, his crib, and his stroller?
    ANSWERS: a. *Angie* by Janice May Udry
    b. *The View from the Cherry Tree* by Willo Davis Roberts
    c. *Pig Pig Grows Up* by David McPhail

Two classes can compete against each other, with a one-, two-, and three-point round. Teams alternate reading questions; points are given only for correct answers. Teachers should call on volunteers and award a bonus point for each author identified.

Professional Bibliography

Overview of Children's Literature: Texts

Huck, Charlotte. *Children's Literature in the Elementary School.* 3rd ed., updated. Holt, 1979.
(A thorough study, encompassing every aspect of developing a literature program.)

Lukens, Rebecca J. *A Critical Handbook of Children's Literature.* 2nd. ed. Scott, Foresman, 1982.
(How to evaluate children's books in terms of genre, characters, plot, setting, theme, point of view, style, and tone.)

Sadker, Myra and David Miller. *Now Upon a Time: A Contemporary View of Children's Literature.* Harper, 1977.
(A thematic approach, divided into modern issues of race, family matters, and world problems.)

Sutherland, Zena, et al. *Children and Books.* Scott, Foresman, 1981.
(Under each genre, the major authors and their works are discussed in detail.)

Reading, Writing, and Booktalking: Ideas and Annotations

Bauer, Caroline Feller. *This Way to Books.* Illus. by Lynn Gates. H.W. Wilson, 1982.
(A grand, attractive collection of book-related projects for all occasions.)

Bodart, Joni. *Booktalk!: Booktalking and School Visiting for Young Adult Audiences.* H.W. Wilson, 1980.
(Even though the focus is on teenagers, the first half of the book, discussing the whys and hows of booktalking, applies to all levels.)

Carlson, Ruth Kearney. *Enrichment Ideas: Sparking Fireflies.* 2nd. ed. Wm. C. Brown, 1976.
(Hundreds of suggestions for extending the classroom reading program with children's books.)
————. *Writing Aids Through the Grades.* Teachers College Press, 1970.
(Developmental activities for writing poetry and prose.)

Cullinan, Bernice E., and Carmichael, Carolyn, eds. *Literature and Young Children.* NCTE, 1977.
(Sensible strategies for presenting books to children. Includes bibliographies after each chapter and a list of one hundred best books and authors for young children.)

Illustration from GRANFA' GRIG HAD A PIG AND OTHER RHYMES WITHOUT REASON FROM MOTHER GOOSE, illustrated by Wallace Tripp. Copyright © 1976 by Wallace Tripp. Reproduced by permission of Little, Brown and Company.

Dreyer, Sharon Spredemann. *The Bookfinder: A Guide to Children's Literature about the Needs and Problems of Youth Aged 2–15; Volumes 1 and 2.* American Guidance Service, 1977 and 1981.
(Indexed by subject, these are enormous, well-annotated bibliographies of children's books that can be used for bibliotherapy.)

Edwards, Margaret A. *The Fair Garden and the Swarm of Beasts: The Library and the Young Adult.* Hawthorn, 1969.
(For older children, but includes excellent practical advice on booktalking.)

The Elementary School Library Collection: A Guide to Books and Other Media. 13th. ed. Bro-Dart, 1982.
(An enormous annotated catalogue, issued yearly, of suggested new and favorite titles for children. Arranged like a library shelf list, i.e., non-fiction in Dewey order, fiction and easy in alphabetical order by author, etc. Includes copious indexes, reference and AV material, subject headings for each entry—in short, an indispensible tool for librarians.)

Gillespie, John T. *More Juniorplots: A Guide for Teachers and Librarians.* Bowker, 1977.
(Includes a marvelous first chapter on booktalking by Mary K. Chelton and booktalk material for seventy-two novels for grades five and up.)

Gillespie, John, and Lembo, Diana. *Introducing Books: A Guide for the Middle Grades.* Bowker, 1970.
(Thematically arranged, generously annotated guide for booktalkers. Each of the more than six dozen book reviews includes plot analysis and thematic booktalk and other suggestions for using the title with children.)

————. *Juniorplots: A Booktalk Manual for Teachers and Librarians.* Bowker, 1977.
(Uses the same format as *Introducing Books,* above.)

Kimmel, Margaret Mary, and Segel, Elizabeth. *For Reading Out Loud! A Guide to Sharing Books with Children.* Delacorte, 1983.
(Full-page detailed write-ups of 140 good books to read aloud, with advice on how to do it.)

Larrick, Nancy. *A Parent's Guide to Children's Reading.* 4th. ed. Doubleday, 1983.
(Hundreds of suggested titles and activities to try at home.)

Leonard, Charlotte. *Tied Together: Topics and Thoughts for Introducing Children's Books.* Scarecrow, 1980.

(Hundreds of titles, with ways to present them to children.)

Paulin, Mary Ann. *Creative Uses of Children's Literature*. Library Professional Publications, 1982.
(A vast compendium of ideas.)

Polette, Nancy. *Nancy Polette's E Is for Everybody: A Manual for Bringing Fine Picture Books into the Hands and Hearts of Children*. 2nd. ed. Scarecrow, 1982.
(Annotations and activities for 126 picture books; includes a section on interpreting literature through art and media.)

Reasoner, Charles F. *Releasing Children to Literature*. Dell, 1976.

————. *Where the Readers Are*. Dell, 1972.
(Teaching units using Dell paperbacks for independent reading. For each annotated title, there are pre- and postreading discussion questions and suggested activities.)

Sloan, Glenna Davis. *The Child as Critic: Teaching Literature in the Elementary School*. Teachers College Press, 1975.
(Includes a fascinating explanation of literary imagery and the four types of literature: comedy, romance, tragedy, and irony-satire.)

Trelease, Jim. *The Read-Aloud Handbook*. Penguin, 1982.
(Why and what to read aloud; a treasury of over three hundred annotated titles.)

Zavatsky, Bill, and Padgett, Ron, eds. *The Whole Word Catalog 2*. McGraw, 1977.
(A myriad of creative ideas for writing poetry and prose.)

Storytelling and Creative Dramatics

Baker, Augusta, and Greene, Ellin. *Storytelling: Art and Technique*. Bowker, 1977.
(A sensible manual for beginning and experienced storytellers alike.)

Bauer, Caroline Feller. *Handbook for Storytellers*. American Library Association, 1977.
(A gold mine of ideas, from planning to delivery.)

Bettelheim, Bruno. *The Uses of Enchantment: The Meaning and Importance of Fairy Tales*. Knopf, 1976.
(Fascinating interpretations by the famous child psychologist. "Little Red Riding Hood" will never be the same.)

Chambers, Dewey W. *The Oral Tradition: Storytelling and Creative Drama*. 2nd. ed. Wm. C. Brown, 1977.
(A useful guide, laced with practical suggestions for working with children.)

De Wit, Dorothy. *Children's Faces Looking Up: Program Building for the Storyteller.* ALA, 1979.
(Developing storytelling programs on a multitude of themes, with suggestions for tales that tie in.)

Heinig, Ruth Beall, and Stillwell, Lyda. *Creative Drama for the Classroom Teacher.* 2nd. ed. Prentice, 1979.
(A thorough guide, relating children's literature to drama activities.)

Sawyer, Ruth. *The Way of the Storyteller.* Viking, 1962.
(Engrossing commentary on the art by a famous American storyteller, with a sampling of her favorite tales.)

Shedlock, Marie L. *The Art of the Storyteller.* 3rd. ed. Dover, 1951.
(A book of instructions and tales originally published in 1915 by a renowned American storyteller.)

Ziskind, Sylvia. *Telling Stories to Children.* H.W. Wilson, 1976.
(A how-to text for budding storytellers.)

Poetry

Gensler, Kinereth, and Nyhart, Nina. *The Poetry Connection: An Anthology of Contemporary Poems with Ideas to Stimulate Children's Writing.* Teachers & Writers, 1978.
(After hearing what these other children have composed, your students will be raring to write.)

Hopkins, Lee Bennett. *Pass the Poetry, Please!: Using Poetry in Pre-Kindergarten–Six Classrooms.* Citation, 1972.
(More foolproof ideas.)

Koch, Kenneth. *Rose, Where Did You Get That Red?: Teaching Great Poetry to Children.* Random, 1973.
(Koch's conversational descriptions of how he enthralled third through sixth graders with both classic and modern poems will encourage you to follow his lead.)

——————. *Wishes, Lies and Dreams: Teaching Children to Write Poetry.* Chelsea House, 1970.
(Numerous inspired ideas for composing poems, with each type followed by children's written examples.)

Witucke, Virginia. *Poetry in the Elementary School.* Wm. C. Brown, 1970.
(Defining, finding, and utilizing poems; tips for the hesitant educator.)

Folklore and Literature Anthologies

Arbuthnot, May Hill, et al. *The Arbuthnot Anthology of*

Children's Literature. 4th. ed. Revised by Zena Sutherland. Scott, Foresman, 1976.
(A huge collection of poetry and folktales, excerpts from fiction, non-fiction, and biography, and a final section on using literature with children.)

Botkin, B.A. *A Treasury of American Folklore.* Crown, 1944.
(A dandy resource of stories and songs collected in the United States)

Calvino, Italo. *Italian Folktales.* Pantheon, 1980.
(Two hundred tales for all ages, including adults.)

Clarkson, Atelia, and Cross, Gilbert B. *World Folktales: A Scribner Resource Collection.* Scribner, 1980.
(Another large, splendid assortment.)

Cole, Joanna. *Best-Loved Folktales of the World.* Illus. by Jill Karla Schwarz. Doubleday, 1982.
(Two hundred tales, from obscure to old favorites.)

Grimm, Jacob and Wilhelm. *The Complete Grimm's Fairy Tales.* Illus. by Josef Scharl. Pantheon, 1972.
(All 210 stories collected by the German folklorists in the first half of the nineteenth century.)

Johnson, Edna, et al. *Anthology of Children's Literature.* 4th. ed. Illus. by Fritz Eichenberg. Houghton, 1970.
(A voluminous collection of poetry, folktales, myths, fiction, biography, and then some, including notes on storytelling and a history of children's literature.)

Power, Effie Louise. *Bag O' Tales: A Source Book for Storytellers.* Gale, 1934.
(An old treasure-packed collection of folktales.)

Illustration from SCARY STORIES TO TELL IN THE DARK by Alvin Schwartz. Text copyright © 1981 by Alvin Schwartz. Illustrations copyright © 1981 by Stephen Gammell. Reproduced by permission of Harper & Row, Publishers, Inc.

AUTHOR INDEX

TITLE INDEX